HENRY ELLIOT MALDEN

SALUS VIENNA TUA
THE GREAT SIEGE OF 1683

WITNESS TO HISTORY 003

SOLDIERSHOP
PUBLISHING

AUTHOR:

Henry Elliot Malden (8 May 1849-1931), already secretary of the Royal Historical Societyr. He was a modest and retiring scholar, who neither sought nor received the credit he deserved for his learning. From Queen Elizabeth's School, Ipswich, he went up to Trinity Hall, Cambridge, where he rowed in the first Hall boar for five years and was president of the Hall Boat Club. There was no Historical Tripos in those days, and Malden took a second class in the Classical Tripos in 1872. He won the Chancellor's Meal for English verse in 1871. He devoted himself largely to the intricacies of local history. He was a prominent member of the Surrey Archaeological Society and edited the Victoria History of Surrey, having himself produced an excellent short history of that country, with many other contributions.

PUBLISHING NOTE

WITNESS TO HISTORY

Our book series of history, based on eyewitnesses, or the great storytellers and war correspondents of the great events of world history: battles, sieges, military campaigns, but also travels and discoveries. New books from old books and completely revised and illustrated by Soldiershop!

To my father Amilcare

ISBN: 9788893271097   1st edition July 2016 Ebook edition ISBN 9788896519844

Title: - **SALUS VIENNA TUA - The great siege of 1683 (WTH-003)**
by Henry Elliot Malden (1833-1904). Revised and enriched by Luca Stefano Cristini (note & illustrations) Editor: Soldiershop publishing - Cover & Art Design: Luca S. Cristini.

Cover: The battle of Wien, September, 1683

PREFACE

Asplendid book this"Salus Vienna Tua", from the orginal work of British historian Henry Elliot Malden thet provides a detailed account of the intricate machinations between the Habsburgs and the Ottomans. Malden's description of the siege itself is masterly and always a fresh reading. Very clearly are the detail of the negotiations among the Christian princes and charting the march of the various armies. He seems to know every inch of ground, every earthwork and fortification around the Imperial City, and he follows the action meticulously. Very enriched by several wonderful colour plates of Allies and Turkish soldiers and a lot of other images. The failure of the Turkish army to take Vienna in 1683 marks the beginning of the long decline of the Ottoman state but it was a close-run affair. Kara Mustafa's janissaries laid siege to the Austrian imperial capital while allied horsemen ravaged the surrounding countryside. Leopold III and his court had fled leaving the rescue of Vienna to Charles, Duke of Lorraine and John Sobieski of Poland. Another good issue, a fine story teller of our series witness to history

This book is based on"*Vienna 1683 The History And Consequences Of The Defeat Of The Turks Before Vienna, September 12, 1683 By John Sobieski, King Of Poland And Charles Leopold, Duke Of Lorraine*"By Henry Elliot Malden London Regan Paul, Trexcii & Co, 1, Paternoster Square 1883. The colour plate of Turkish and Polish soldiers are originally artworks of Soldiershop ©.
No effort has been made to modernize or standardize the spelling used in the original text.

Original Preface

The historical scholar will find nothing new in the following pages; but I have thought it worth while to tell to the general reader a story worth the telling, and to explain not only the details, but the wider bearings also, of a great crisis in European history, no satisfactory account of which exists, I believe, in English, and the two hundredth anniversary of which is now upon us. My principal authorities are *"Sobieski's Letters to his Queen,"* edited by Count Plater, Paris, 1826; Starhemberg's *"Life and Despatches,"* edited by Count Thurheim, Vienna, 1882; *"Campaigns of Prince Eugene, of Savoy,"* Vienna, 1876, etc.; Schimmer's *"Sieges of Vienna;"* Von Hammer 's *"History of the Turks;"* Salvandy's"History of Poland; *"Memoirs of . Eugene"* by De Ligne; *"Memoirs of Charles, Duke of Lorraine, and his Military Maxims,"* published late in the seventeenth century; *"Works of Montecuccoli;"* De la Guillatiere's *"View of the Present State of the Turkish Empire, etc,"* translated, London, 1676, etc. I have been obliged to reject some statements of Salvandy's, such, for instance, as that the crescent moon was eclipsed on the day of the battle before Vienna.

I regret that I have been unable to use the account of the campaign of 1683 published in Vienna, by the Director of the War Archives, since this went to press. Some of the matter of it is, I believe, contained in the *"Campaigns of Eugene,"* published under the same authority mentioned above, and in Schimmer's work.

Henry Elliot Malden

CONTENTS:

"Think of that age's awful birth,
When Europe echoed, terror-riven,
That a new foot was on the earth,
And a new name come down from Heaven
When over Calpe's straits and steeps
The Moor had bridged his royal road,
And Ottoman's sons from Asia's deeps
The conquests of the Cross overflowed.

"Think with what passionate delight
The tale was told in Christian halls,
How Sobieski turned to flight
The Muslim from Vienna's walls;
How, when his horse triumphant trod
The burghers' richest robes upon,
The ancient words rose loud, " From God
A man was sent whose name was John!"

LORD HOUGUION.

SYNOPSIS OF EVENTS

1663. Ahmed Kiuprili Grand Vizier.

1664. Montecuculi defeats the Turks at St. Gotthard. Twenty years' truce with Austria, by which the Turks retain most of Hungary.

1669. The Turks take Candia from the Venetians.

1671. Conspiracy in Hungary against the Emperor crushed.

1672. French attack upon Holland provokes a general war. Treaty of Buksacs between the Turks and Poles. Poland cedes most of Podolia and the Ukraine, and pays tribute to Turkey.

1673. The Polish nobles break the treaty. Great victory of Sobieski over the Turks at Choczim.

1675. Sobieski crowned King of Poland.

1676. Treaty of Zurawna between Turks and Poles; the former retain most of their conquests.

1677. Death of Ahmed Kiuprili. Kara Mustapha Grand Vizier.

1678. Tekeli heads an insurrection in Hungary against the Emperor. The French intrigue with him.

1678-79. Treaties of Nimuegen between the French and the allies.

1681. Louis XIV. Seizes Strassburg and makes other aggressions upon the Empire. Treaty between Holland and Sweden against France.

1682. Treaty of Laxenberg between the Emperor and the Upper German Circles against France, followed by similar treaties between the other Circles, the Emperor and Sweden. The Turks openly aid the Hungarians.

1683. League of the Empire, Poland and the Pope, supported by other anti-French powers, against the Turks. Turkish invasion of Austria. Siege of Vienna. Defeat of the Turks by John Sobieski and the Duke of Lorraine, September 12. The French attack the Spanish Netherlands in the autumn.

1684. Truce of Ratisbon between France and the Empire.

1686. Buda recovered from the Turks. League of Augsburg between the Emperor and the Circles of Western Germany, joined ultimately by Spain, Holland, the Pope, Savoy and other Princes of the Empire, against the French.

1688. The English Revolution secures England for the side of the League, which she joins next year. General war with France follows.

1696. Death of Sobieski.

1697. Treaty of Ryswick between France and the allies. Eugene defeats the Turks at Zenta, in Hungary.

1699. Peace of Carlowitz. The Turks cede nearly all Hungary, Transylvania, Podolia, the Ukraine, the Morea and Azof.

The first great diminution of Turkish territory in Europe.

MAHOMETUS QUARTUS IMPERATOR TURCARIUM. IOANNES CASIMIRVS DEI GRACIA REX POLO: NIÆ AC SV ECIÆ. &c.

▲ The two adversaries king: Mhoammed IV and Jan Sobiesky

CHAPTER I

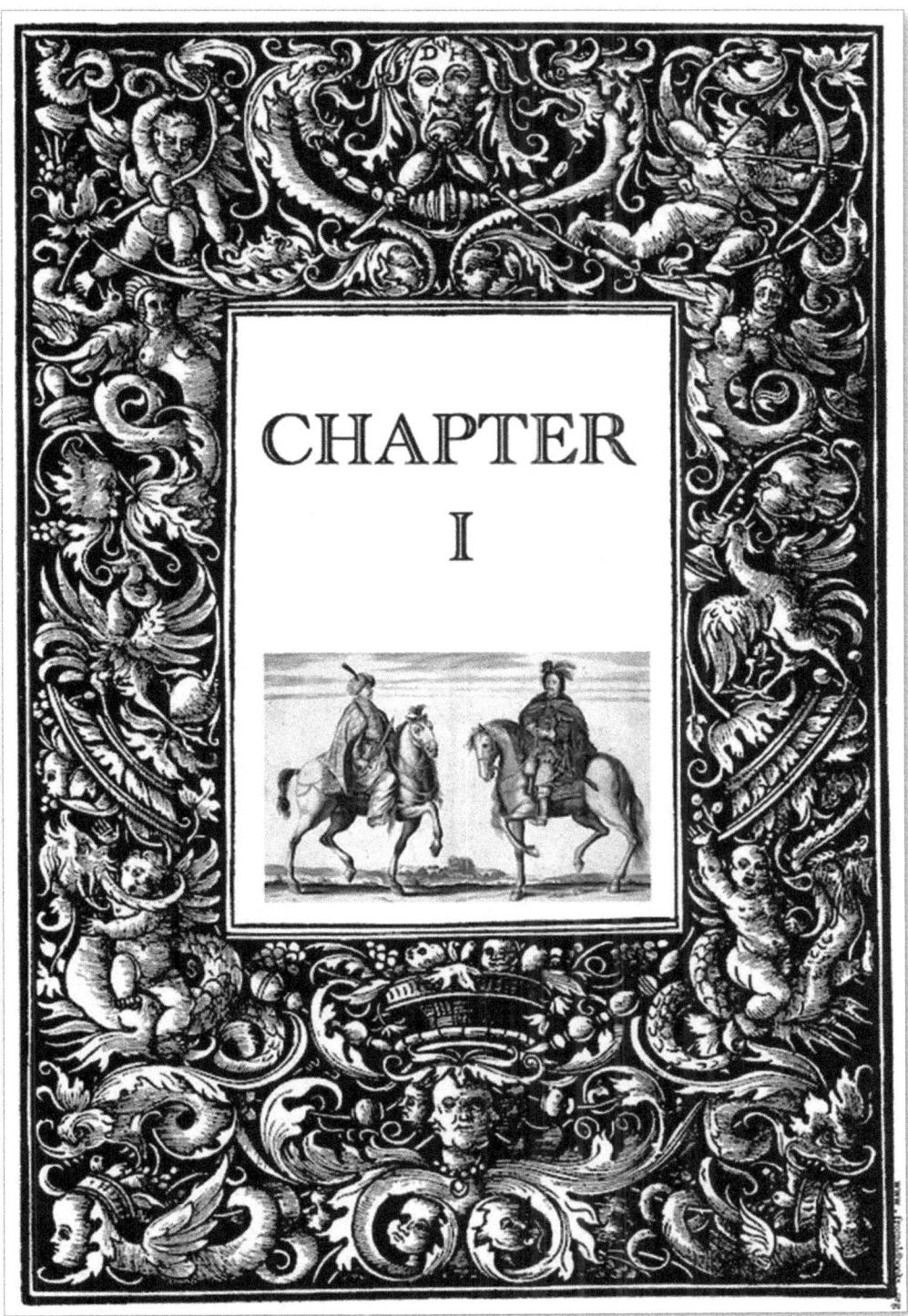

▲ The empire in the Turkish storm....

CHAPTER I - VIENNA 1683

At the present moment, in 1883, the power of Austria is driven as a wedge into the midst of the former dominions of the Sultan. That this is so, perhaps that Austria even exists as a great power, and can hope to be a greater in south-eastern Europe, is owing in no small degree to the Polish aid which in 1683 defeated the Turkish armies before the gates, and saved Vienna. The victor, John Sobieski, King of Poland, then deserved and enjoyed the gratitude of Christendom. But the unequal fate of a man great in character and in abilities, but born out of due time, in an incongruous age and in a state unworthy of him, has seldom been more conspicuously illustrated than in his career. The great men of the last quarter of the seventeenth century whom we most readily remember are men of western Europe. Louis XIV, with the resources of France behind him, William III, wielding the power of England, of Holland, and of Protestant Germany, are the kings who fill the stage. The half-crazy hero, Charles XII. of Sweden, is a more familiar character than the great Polish king, the deliverer first of Poland, secondly of Germany, perhaps of Europe.

The causes are not far to seek. The country which he ruled has disappeared from the roll of European nations. The enemy whom he defeated has become, in his last decrepitude, the object merely of scorn, or of not disinterested care. It seems now so incredible that the Turks should have been a menace to Europe, that it is no great claim to remembrance to have defeated them. Sobieski, too, in his greatness and in his weakness, was a medieval hero. He was out of place in the age of Louis XIV.

He was a great soldier rather than a great general, a national hero rather than a great king. His faith had the robust sincerity of that of a thirteenth-century knight, his character was marred by the violent passions of a medieval baron. His head was full of crusading projects of the expulsion of the Turks, of the revival of a Catholic Greek state, not without principalities for his own house.

His plans would have commanded support in the days of St. Louis, but were impracticable in a Europe whose rulers schemed for a balance of power. Poland herself perished, partly through clinging to a medieval constitution in the midst of modern states. Her medievally-minded king and his exploits are eclipsed by other memories, even upon the scene of his greatest achievement.

For the traveller who from the Tower of St. Stephen's, in the centre of the old-town of Vienna, looks down upon the places made remarkable by great historic actions in the valley of the Danube, has his eye turned first northward and eastward upon the Marchfeld. There, he is told, are Aspern and Essling, where the Archduke Charles beat Napoleon in 1809. There is the island of Lobau, where Napoleon repaired his forces, and whence he issued to fight yonder the great and terrible conflict of Wagram.

The scene, not of a greater slaughter, not of a more obstinately contested fight, than Wagram, but the scene of a battle more momentous in its consequences, lies upon the other side. Among the vineyards, villages, and chateaux which cover the lower slopes of the Wiener Wald, among the suburbs of Nussdorf and of Hernals, Charles of Lorraine and John Sobieski smote the Turkish armies in 1683.

There at one blow they frustrated the last great Mohammedan aggression against Christendom, and set free the minds and arms of the Germans to combine against French ambition upon their western frontier. The victory was one of those decisive events which complete long pending revolutions, and inaugurate new political conditions in Europe.

The treaties of Nimuegen in 1678-79 had marked a pause in a general European contest. France and the Empire, Holland, Spain, Sweden, Brandenburg, all retired from their active conflicts, to plot and strive in secret, till an advantageous opening for war should again present itself

Poland and the Porte had a little earlier concluded their strife by the peace of Zurawna. But in the general breathing-time the eyes of all were turned with anxiety upon Eastern Europe.

So much of Hungary as was not in the hands of the Sultan was in insurrection against the Emperor. The insolence of the Turks, and their support to the insurgents, were continually becoming greater.

The whole East resounded with warlike preparations, and it was without doubt evident that a great enterprise "Was being prepared which might make the reign of Mahomet IV as illustrious for Islam, as calamitous for Christendom, as that of Mahomet II. had been. Rome, Venice, Vienna, were the three capitals in more immediate danger, but the whole continent "Was interested, and all other designs were necessarily suspended till it became clearer where this storm would fall, and what resistance could be made to it.

For, two hundred years ago, the Ottoman Empire still stood high among the greatest of European powers. Spain ruled over wider territories; but the dominions of Spain were scattered over the Old and New Worlds, and her European lands, in the Netherlands and in Italy, were divided from her by the sea, or isolated by the interposition of the frontiers of powerful and often hostile neighbors.

A compact yet widely spread collection of kingdoms and of provinces obeyed the head of the Mohammedan world. Northern Africa, Western Asia, Eastern Europe were ruled from the Bosporus. All the chief centres of ancient civilization, Rome alone excepted, Thebes, Nineveh and Babylon, Carthage, Athens and Constantinople, bowed beneath the Crescent. The southern frontiers of the Sultan's territories reached beyond the Tropic of Cancer, the northern touched nearly the latitude of Paris.

The modern kingdoms of Greece, Serbia, Romania were wholly his; the kingdom of Hungary, the dominions of Austria and of Russia were in part his also. The Black Sea was entirely encircled with Turkish or tributary territory; no other power possessed the same extent of coast line on the Mediterranean.

Not only the Euphrates, the Tigris, the Nile, but the Danube, the Boug, the Dneister, the Dneiper and the Don flowed for a great part of their course between banks subject or tributary to the Porte, and reached the sea by mouths wholly under Turkish control. The armies of the Sultan were unapproachable in numbers, unsurpassable in valour, by those of the Christian powers. Their discipline and warlike science were no longer what they once had been, the first in Europe; but their inequality in these respects to their enemies was not yet so marked as at present.

Military and administrative skill were yet to be found in their empire. From the first appearance of the Turks in Europe Mohammedan rule had been, on the whole, extending. The Christian reconquest of Spain was balanced by the inroads of this new enemy upon the Eastern Empire.

The Spanish reconquest of Grenada, in the fifteenth century, was more than counterbalanced by the Turkish conquest of Hungary in the sixteenth. The Turks upon the middle Danube were a menace at once to Poland, Germany, and to northern Italy. Nor was this a mere temporary inroad of theirs. Two-thirds of Hungary were then more firmly held in their grasp than Macedonia is at present, and their frontiers were not going back.

In the seventeenth century the Ottoman power still more than held its own in Eastern Europe. Though the Spaniards and Venetians had destroyed their fleet at Lepanto in 1571, though Montecuccoli at the head of the Imperial troops had routed their armies at St. Gotthard in 1664, though Sobieski and the Poles made the great slaughter of Choczim in 1673, yet the frontiers of the Turks were advanced by every war.

After Lepanto, the peace confirmed them in the possession of the newly acquired Cyprus; after St. Gotthard, they retained the strong city of Neuhausel, which they had just won, in Hungary, and conquered Candia; after Choczim, they were confirmed in possession of the province of Podolia, and their supremacy over the Ukraine, the Marchland of Poland. Of theil' soldiers the most formidable were the Janissaries.

The policy of the earlier' Sultans had demanded a tribute of boys from their Christian subjects. These children, early converts to Islam, were brought up with no home but the camp, no occupation but war ; and, under the title of Janissaries, or the New Troops, were alternately the servants and the masters of the Ottoman Sultans. The strength of the Christians as drained, the strength of the Ottoman armies multiplied, and the fields of Paradise l'eplenished at once, in the judgment of pious Mussllmans, by this policy. At this time the ranks of the Janissaries were not solely filled by this levy, but it has been computed that 500,000 Christian boys may have become instruments for the subjugation of Christendom, from the first institution of the tax in the fourteenth century clown to the final levy made in 1675.

Our commiseration for the Christian parents may be mitigated by the consideration that to sell their children into slavery, uncompelled, was a not unknown practice among the subjects of the Eastern Emperors, before the Mohammedan conquest. These Janissaries formed a disciplined body of regular infantry.

In the seventeenth century the Turks clung to the sabre, the musket, and even bows and arrows, as their arms, neglecting the pike, "the queen of infantry weapons" as Montecuccoli calls it, just as afterwards they neglected the bayonet. But in the use of their arms every man of the Janissaries was a trained expert.

The Turkish horsemen were famed for their rapidity of action, being generally more lightly armed and better mounted than the Germans or Poles. The Spahis, or royal horseguards, were the flower of the cavalry.

The feudal levy from lands held by military tenure, swelled the numbers of their armies, and every province wrested from the Christians provided more fiefs to support fresh families of soldiers. Thus the children and lands of the conquered furnished the means for new conquests. Light troops, who were expected to live by plunder, spread far and wide before an advancing Ottoman host, eating up the country, destroying the inhabitants, and diverting the attention of the enemy.

The Ottoman artillery was numerous, and the siege pieces of great calibre. Auxiliaries, such as the Tartars of the Crimea, the troops of Moldavian, Wallachian, Transylvanian, and even Hungarian princes, made a formidable addition to their forces. These armies lay, a terror to the inhabitants, a constant anxiety to the rulers, upon the frontiers of Germany and of Poland; a black storm of war, ever ready to break in destructive energy upon them. Whatever schism divided Turks and Persians, towards Europe at least, from the Caspian to Morocco, Islam presented an unbroken front, contrasting powerfully with the bitter divisions of Christendom. Massinger, in the "Renegade" puts into the mouth of a Moslem what many a Christian must have thought of with shame and terror:

> *"Look on our flourishing empire if the splendour,*
> *The majesty, and glory of it dim not*
> *Your feeble sight; and then turn back and see*
> *The narrow bounds of yours, yet that poor remnant,*
> *Rent in as many factions and opinions*
> *As you have petty kingdoms."*

▲ Portrait of the Capuchin friar Marco d'Aviano (1631 – 1699)

United Islam, which had preceded her western rival Spain in greatness, seemed also destined to long outlive that power's decay. When Spain, in the sixteenth century, had been at the zenith of her power under Charles V, the Turks, under their great Emperor Solyman, had been not unworthy rivals to her.

Even then Solyman had penetrated to the walls of Vienna, in 1529, and probably the lateness of the season, October, and the absence of his heavy artillery, stuck deep in the soil of Hungarian roads, saved the capital of the Austrian dominions more effectually than the valour of the garrison or the relieving forces of Charles could have done.

Then the tide of Turkish power touched its farthest limit, but the fear of its return was not destroyed till after the lapse of one hundred and fifty years. Till after the siege of 1683, it is said that a crescent disgraced the spire of St. Stephen's, the cathedral of Vienna - a sign to avert the fire of Turkish gunners. In the seventeenth century, when the great empire of Spain was fast approaching dissolution, when France was the great power of 'Western Europe, the Turks were still the great power of the East, with territories even more widely extended than in the previous age. It is true that, after the death of Solyman, a series of incapable rulers and the natural decay of an eastern despotism had paralyzed the great powers of Turkey; but the stern reforming vigour of Amurath IV. (1623-40), and, still more, the wise administration of the first two Grand Viziers of the house of Kiuprili, had done much to restore good government, vigour and efficiency to the Ottomans.[1]

Their empire, the speedy downfall of which had been predicted by the English Ambassador, Sir Thomas Roe, at the beginning of the seventeenth century, had since fully recovered its former reputation.

A clever Frenchman, M. de la Guillatiere, who visited the camp of Kiuprili in Candia in 1669, formed the highest estimate of the military genius of the Turks, and of their political insight into the power and designs of the Christians. He judged of the greatness of the Sultan by considering the number and quality of the persons who feared his displeasure. When he makes any great preparation, Malta trembles, Spain is fearful for his kingdoms of Naples and Sicily, the Venetian anxious for what he holds in Greece-Dalmatia and Friuli, the Germans apprehensive for what remains to them in Hungary, Poland is alarmed, and the consternation passes on as far as Muscovy, and, not resting there, expands itself to the Christian princes in Gourgistan and Mingrelia; Persia, Arabia, the Abyssinians are all in confusion, whilst neither man nor woman nor beast in all this vast tract but looks out for refuge till they be certain whither his great force is intended. It is a striking estimate of Turkish power, but not beyond what experience confirmed.

It was not till the second siege of Vienna, and her relief by Sobieski in 1683, that the real instability of the power of the Sultan was disclosed, that his armies were routed, his frontiers curtailed, his power rolled back within the Save and the Carpathians. Not for the first time, in the summer of that year, Europe trembled at the progress of the Crescent. Since then, the tide of victory has run almost uninterruptedly in favour of the Cross, and Turkey has sunk from being the terror to the position of protégée, tool, victim, or tolerated scandal of Europe.

The decline of her forces, the reversal of the former position of Turk and Christian in the East, date from this great catastrophe of Islam. For Eastern Europe at least the battle before Vienna was a decisive battle.

We must remember, indeed, what is meant by a decisive battle, or by any other so-called decisive event.

They are rather the occasions than the causes of the transference of power. The causes lie deep which can produce such great and such lasting results. The operation of many influences, throughout a length of time, brings about ultimately the striking revolutions in the history of mankind. No chance bullet which strikes down, or avoids, a commander; no brilliant display of military genius in the person of one man; no incapacity of a single officer, can do more than alter the minor circumstances of great events. The great man is not successfully great, unless his genius can seize upon the opportunities offered by a rising tide of popular opinion, or profit by the accumulated energy of a nation. The incapable leader can seldom make shipwreck of a power unless it be built upon unsafe lines.

The presence of a thoroughly incapable commander argues something rotten in his cause. The revolution, the

---

1- Ahmed Kiuprili, the second Vizier of his race, was one of the greatest ministers of bis day. He was described by the Turkish historians as "the light and splendour of the nation, the preserver and administrator of good laws, tbe vicar of the shadow of God, the thrice learned and all accomplished Grand Vizier." He seems to have really deserved some of the praise.

reformation, the reaction, the transference of empire will come; if not in one way, in another; if not in one year, in the next, or in following years. The foundations of success and of failure, are laid deep in the moral, religious and political habits and institutions of nations. The invincible determination and high political and military training of the Roman aristocracy bore them safely through the catastrophes of a Second Punic War and the revolt of their allies. The ordered liberty, and the generations of successful adventure, which were the heritage of the English nation, had won Trafalgar before a shot had been fired from the Victory.

The Persian host went forth predestined to choke the Gulf of Salamis with corpses. No Kosciusko's valour could redeem the long anarchy and blindness of Poland. Napoleon, marching from victory to victory, but approached the nearer to that fall, which must await one man against a continent in arms.

So the Turkish myriads, victorious at Vienna, would have fallen upon some less noble field before the skill of some other Sobieski. But the genius and courage of individuals may well determine the fate of armies for a day. One day's victory may call for years of warfare to accomplish its undoing.

A few years of delay may work great changes in the fortunes of men. It is no mistaken estimate of the relative value of causes, it is no unintelligent interest which makes us prone to linger over the one dramatic moment that moment when the courses of the tendencies of ages are declared within the compass of a day.

By no hard effort of imagination we identify our interest with that of the actors in the scene.

To them, however confident, the result is never clear; to them the delay of a few years in the overthrow of some inevitably falling wrong may make that difference for which no ultimate success can compensate.

It was cold comfort to the inhabitants of Vienna, or to the King of Poland, to know that even if St. Stephen's had shared the fate of St. Sophia and become a mosque of Allah, and if the Polish standards had been borne in triumph to the Bosphorus, yet that, nevertheless, the undisciplined Ottomans would infallibly have been scattered by French, German and Swedish armies on the fields of Bavaria or of Saxony. Vienna would have been sacked; Poland would have been a prey to internal anarchy and to Tartar invasion.

The ultimate triumph of their cause would have consoled few for their individual destruction.

Prompted by feelings such as these we dwell upon the decisive hours, when the long assured superiority asserts itself, for good and all. We can hail Marathon, Salamis, Tours, or Vienna as the occasion, if not the cause, of the triumph of civilization over barbarism, of Europe over Asia. We must remember, too, that, if the day for a permanent advance of Turkish power was over, yet that a temporary Turkish victory, and a protracted war in Germany, could not have been confined in their influence to the seat of war alone. So cool and experienced a diplomatist as Sir William Temple did indeed believe, at the time, that the fall of Vienna would have been followed by a great and permanent increase of Turkish power.[2]

Putting this aside however, there were other results likely to spring from Turkish success.

The Turks constantly made a powerful diversion in favour of France and her ambitious designs.

Turkish victories upon the one side of Germany meant successful French aggressions upon the other, and Turkish schemes were promoted with that object by the French The author of the memoirs of Prince Eugene writes bitterly, but truly enough, of this crisis: *"Le roi tres chretien avant d'etre devot, secourait les chretiens contre les infideles (at St. Gotthard and at Candia), devenu pourtant un grand homme de bien, il les agacait contre l'empereur, et soutenait les rebelles de Hongrie. Sans lui ils ne seraient jamais venus, les uns et les autres, aux portes de Vienne".* "

If France would but stand neutral, the controversy between Turks and Christians might soon be decided" says the Duke of Lorraine. But France would not stand neutral.

2- If the Turks had possessed this bulwark of Christendom (Vienna), I do not conceive what could have hindered them from being masters immediately of Austria, and all its depending provinces; nor, in another year, of all Italy, or of the southern provinces of Germany, as they should have chosen to carry on their invasion, or of both in two or three years' time; and how fatal this might have been to the rest of Christendom, or how it might have enlarged the Turkish dominions, is easy to conjecture. -Sir W. Temple, Works, iii. 393, edit. 1814.

▲ Polish-Lithuanian Hetman Distinctive hetman's symbol was the mace bulawa, both in military operations and social occasions. Under the cloak lined with fur, wearing a Turkish-inspired chainmail shirt, strengthened on the chest by an husaria lamellar armor and on the forearms by the sarekawie.
Belonging to the highest ranks of the Polish-Lithuanian nobility, the hetman always sported a sophisticated luxury in dress and in the hat trimmed with fur.

CHAPTER II

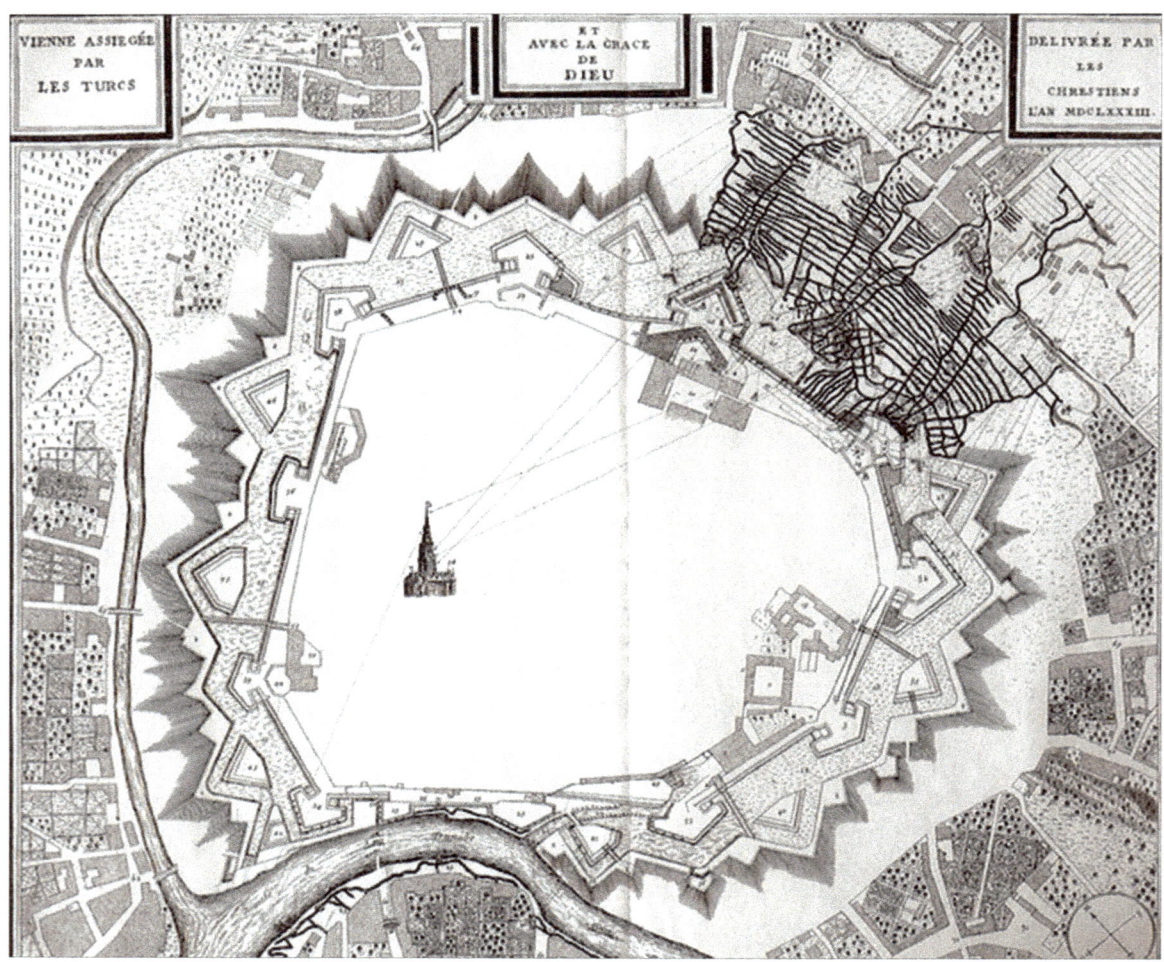

VIENNE ASSIEGÉE PAR LES TURCS — ET AVEC LA GRACE DE DIEU — DELIVRÉE PAR LES CHRESTIENS L'AN MDCLXXXIII.

▲ A French map of Vienna fortifications in the late XVII century.

CHAPTER II

The Emperor was exposed on either side to these two implacable enemies. At Versailles, as at the Porte, had the destruction of the house of Austria been sworn But France was the power which, in the latter half of the seventeenth century, menaced most seriously the independence of her neighbours.

Turkey was, perhaps, from her internal weakness and faulty constitution, in no condition to effect a lasting conquest, however great her mere destructive energies might be. An ingenious nation and an ambitious king, able ministers and skilful generals, revenues, ships, colonies, commercial enterprise, a central situation among divided foes, combined to render France the dominant power of the age.

The great Turkish Vizier, the restorer of order and prosperity, Ahmed Kiuprili, had had a greater counterpart in the French minister, Cardinal Richelieu. The Sultan, Mahomet IV, was wanting in all those qualities which made Louis XIV for long the successful administrator of a despotic power.

The armies of France, under the leadership of a Condé, a Turenne, a Luxembourg, were the finest of the world, the envy of neighbouring princes, the pattern for all soldiers.

The Duke of Marlborough and John Sobieski both learnt their first lessons in military affairs under French command. Prince Eugene vainly sought employment in the French troops; their opposition to himself taught William III. the art of war. Nor was the French ascendency won by arms alone.

The order and splendour of her government, the genius of her authors, the attractions of her society, the diplomatic skill of her ambassadors, made a French party in every court in Europe. Portugal may be said to have owed her independent existence to France; Holland till 1672 ranked as a French ally; Sweden, too far removed to be a rival, was an almost constant friend, till Louis' aggressions alienated her also in 1681.

France had a party in Poland; the petty princes and republics of Italy vacillated between her and the Empire; in England she had had Cromwell as an ally, and she held both Charles II and his opponents in her pay. She maintained an understanding with Turkey.

Discontented Romanists in England and Ireland, unruly Protestants in Hungary, were alike taught to look to her for advice and for assistance. Her frontiers were steadily advancing at the expense of Spain and of the German princes. Neither force nor treaties seemed to avail aught against her superior strength and cunning.

The Lotharingian bishoprics and their dependencies; Elsass, Breisach and Bar, Roussillon, Franche Comté, parts of Flanders, of Artois, of Hainault and Luxemburg, the free imperial city of Strasbourg, the territory of Orange, were steadily absorbed by her, and thoroughly incorporated with the French kingdom.

Her opponents saw no possibility of resistance, save in a great confederacy against her. Her power was not finally checked, nor her ambition confined within bounds, till such a confederacy was made. But it is hardly too much to say that such a confederacy would have been scarcely possible had the Turks been completely victorious at Vienna in 1683.

Three years later than that deliverance, in 1686, the League of Augsburg was formed. It was ultimately the union of the Emperor, the German princes, Sweden, Spain, Holland and the Pope, against an ambition that menaced all.

This League was the basis of that Grand Alliance which finally defeated France under Marlborough and Eugene. But the true foundations of a similar alliance had been laid before, in 1682, principally by the endeavours of the Prince of Waldeck, in the treaty of Laxenberg between the Circles of Upper Germany and the Emperor.

This incipient League against France had been practically suspended by the Turkish invasion. A Turkish success must have dissolved it.

The Pope had been zealous in forming the "Holy League" against the Turks and in promoting union against France. Had Vienna fallen, fear of the Sultan would have driven him into the arms of Louis, and he would have drawn the Catholic powers at least along with him. Probably all the States united in the "Holy League" must have demanded French support for their own salvation. With Austria and Poland beaten, France, and France alone, could have assumed the leadership of Europe against the East. The German Protestant princes would have been ranged under the command of Luxembourg and of Vendome; Louis would have triumphed upon the Danube; the house of Austria would have existed only by the sufferance of her ancient enemy; and French influence would have been riveted, as a chain, by the force of admiration and of gratitude, upon the neck of Europe. Such an event Louis expected, and the Emperor feared.

As the Turks drew near, the French armies lay ready upon the frontier, ready to take advantage of the approaching catastrophe-ready to avenge, but not to save the Empire. We in England, safe as we were from Turkish invasion, were by no means unaffected by the struggle. Nothing which tended to increase or diminish the power of France or of the German princes could be indifferent to us, and at that particular time our fortunes were closely bound up with those of the powers opposing France.

The motive which induced the Dutch government and the other allies of Augsburg to sanction the descent of William III upon our shores, and to withdraw, at a critical moment, the flower of their forces upon such a doubtful enterprise, was the necessity of including England in their league.

Though James II would no doubt have awakened resistance in some form or other anyhow, the plot which actually overthrew him was hatched abroad among the allies, and executed by the help of foreign troops and foreign money. English men, ships, and money were needed to beat the French.

No method was open for obtaining them except by the superseding of King James, entirely or practically, by William, as king or regent. No personal aims nor admiration of Whig principles would have justified the risks William ran. In truth, neither the allies nor the Dutch government would have allowed him to run such risk at all, save for the common good of the League and of Europe. But a Turkish victory at Vienna would have meant the probable non-existence of the League, by the rallying of half its members to the side of France.

It would certainly have meant such a change of circumstances upon the continent, as would have rendered it highly improbable that an army, principally furnished from Germany, could be spared to go to England.

James and the Whig nobility would have fought their quarrel alone, with the High-Church Tory majority of the country as arbiters of the strife. Therefore, had the battle of Vienna been fought differently, the Boyne, La Hogue and Blenheim might never have been fought at all. Forces supplied by England, or paid by England, commanded by Marlborough at Blenheim and at Ramilies, broke French power.

The power of making the alliance which fought at Blenheim and at Ramilies was won at Vienna. To turn to Sir William Temple's views again, so convinced was he that a Turkish invasion of Austria would tend to the great advantage of France, that he believed that the Turks themselves would see it, and for that very reason refrain from the enterprise; it being against their interest to make anyone Christian power so strong as France would then become.[3]

It is certain that Louis XIV fully appreciated the value of that diversion of their attention from himself, which an attack from Hungary upon the rear of the German powers would cause. It is equally certain that he, the eldest son of the Church, the most Christian King, the persecutor of the Huguenots, had some understanding with Mohammedans and with Hungarian Protestant malcontents. And this, too, at a time when religious passions still ran high; when the forces of Europe were everywhere divided, owing to religious intolerance; when France herself was about to be fatally injured by the Revocation of the Edict of N antes. Louis, however, intrigued as readily with Hungarian Protestants as with Irish Romanists, and the intolerance of the Emperor gave every opportunity for interference.

Indeed, the attacks of the Emperor Leopold upon the religion of some of his Hungarian subjects well nigh proved fatal to Austria. The Protestants preferred Mohammedan rule, which, if contemptuous, may be just, and is not avowedly persecuting, to the oppressions of a court dominated by the Jesuit fathers.

Attempts to Germanize their nation and to override their laws united Hungarians of all religions in a common hostility to Vienna. A dangerous conspiracy, fomented by France, was discovered, and crushed in 1671 by the execution of the principal leaders. But Emerich Count Tekeli, the son of one of the chiefs involved, escaping into Transylvania, threw himself upon the protection of the Turks, and with their assistance commenced a

---

3 - "If the Grand Vizier (Kinprili) be so great a man as he is reputed in politics as well as in arms, he will never consent, by an invasion of Hungary, to make way for the advance of French progress into the Empire, which a conquest of the Low Countries would make easy and obvious; and 80 great accessions (with others that would lie fair and open in the Spanish provinces upon the Mediterranean) would make France a formidable power to the Turk himself, and greater than I suppose he desires to see any in Christendom."-Sir W. Temple, Works, ii. 212, edit. 1814.

guerilla warfare in Hungary. Numbers of the inhabitants, irrespective of their religion, joined his standard. A levy, under French officers, was made even in Poland for the assistance of the insurgents. With the almost open aid of the Pasha of Buda, their operations assumed the character of regular warfare, and they fully held their own against the Imperial generals. It was fortunate for Austria that, just as the obligations of a peace and internal confusion had prevented the Turks from attacking Hungary during the Thirty Years' War, so this rising was not taken advantage of by the Porte, in spite of French solicitations, till after the peace of Nimuegen in 1679.

During the contest with France, from 1673 to 1679, the Polish war had occupied the attention of the Turks, and the Austrian government had been untroubled. They had not at the same time to wage open war with the East and West. Yet even now, though peace nominally continued in Western Europe, France was glad to avail herself of those difficulties of the Court of Vienna, to which she herself was contributing.

Louis seized Strasbourg, and quietly annexed other places by the pretended legal decisions of packed tribunals. He attacked the Spanish Netherlands, and conceived himself to be acting generously in that he refrained from taking Luxemburg. It was enough that Austria should be spared the task of fighting, at the same time, on behalf of Spain against the French, and on her own behalf against the Infidels.

That the house of Bourbon should strive to embarrass the house of Hapsburg, by intrigues in Turkey, in Hungary and in Poland, was but in accord with a traditional policy, which no danger to their common Christendom could be expected to overrule. But 1683 was a year of disaster for Louis.

In that year he lost two of his natural sons, his Queen, and his greatest minister, Colbert. Above all, in that year his designs against the Emperor were destined to be foiled by the interference of Sobieski, the Deus ex machina for Christendom and for the Empire.

▲ *A 1661 portrait of Louis XIV, king of France by Charles le Brun*

▲ The King of Poland Jan Sobieski a Vienna. 2- coat of arms of king of Poland. 3- Officer of Polish winged hussar

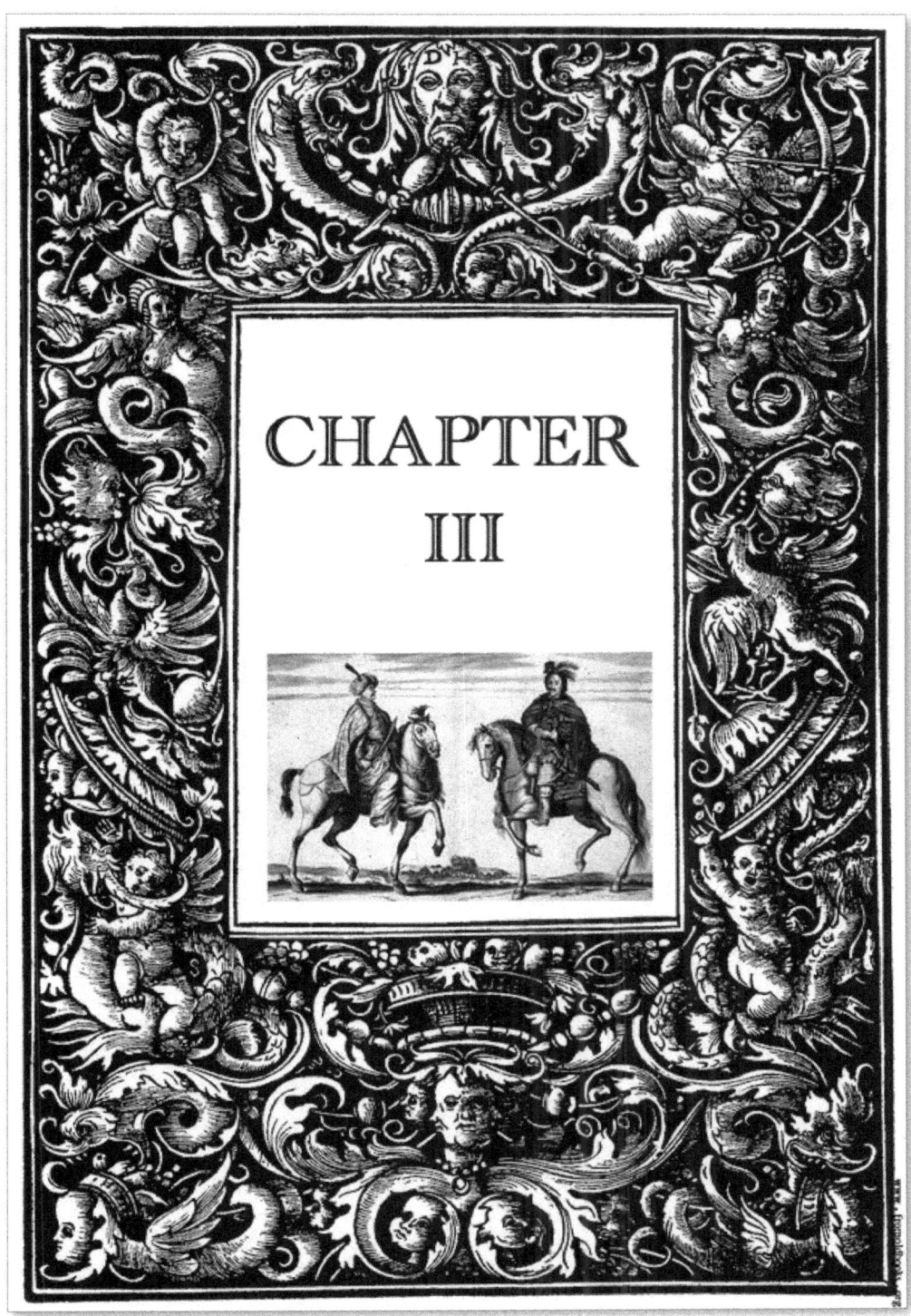

CHAPTER III

▲ The cross head of Saint Stephan church tower with the *"convenient Hottoman reserve head."*

CHAPTER III

To return, therefore, to the troubles in Hungary, which gave occasion for French intrigue and for the interference of the Parte. The Turks, reinvigorated by the policy of the late Vizier Kiuprili, but directed no longer by his cool experience and judgment, were now not slow to take advantage of the difficulties of Austria. After their defeat at the hands of Montecuccoli at St. Gotthard in 1664, they had consented to a twenty years' truce, by which they were still left in possession of the greater part of Hungary, and of that part where the pure Magyar population most prevailed.

This truce had not expired when the oppressions exercised in the part of their country remaining to the Emperor drove the Hungarians to arms, and Count Tekeli to seek aid from the Sultan.

Ordinarily scrupulous in the observance of their treaty obligations, the Turks were on this occasion overcome by the temptations held out to them of an easy extension of their frontier and of their influence.

With the active aid of the Hungarians, and with the tacit consent of France, they deemed it possible to deal a mortal blow at the house of Austria.

The Sultan, Mahomet IV, was perhaps not over ambitious, but he was spurred on by the zeal of a servant.

The Grand Vizier, Rata Mustapha, though a nephew of the great minister Kiuprili, owed his advancement more to the beauty of his person and to the favour of the *Sultana Validé*, or Queen Mother, who ruled the ruler of Islam, than to other connexions or to ability. His ambition, however, was believed to aim at no less than a dependent kingdom for himself in Hungary or at Vienna.

Here, at all events, and not against the Poles or Russians, did Kara Mustapha determine to gather his laurels and his booty. He had, indeed, already essayed a Russian campaign with little profit. A more striking success and greater glories, more abundant plunder with fewer toils, seemed to be promised by a campaign in the valley of the Danube, than by one among the marshes and forests of Poland, or of the Ukraine.

Too late, in 1681, the court of Vienna attempted a conciliatory policy in Hungary. The spirit of rebellion had been aroused, and the offers of redress and justice made by the Emperor were distrusted as a veil for treachery, or despised as the confession of weakness. Tekeli defied the Emperor, and assumed the offensive even beyond the borders of Hungary. Neither was the Porte to be propitiated.

In vain an Imperial Embassy to Constantinople sought a prolongation of the truce, which was on the point of expiring at the end of the stipulated twenty years. The demands of the Turks rose with the progress of their preparations. A principality for their ally, Count Tekeli, in Hungary; extension of territory, with the strongest border fortresses for themselves; a great war indemnity-such were the terms which implied a determination not to negotiate. The ambassador, Count Caprara, was compelled as a prisoner himself to witness the departure of the Turkish hosts for the frontier. At the end of the year 1682 the main body were drawn together at Adrianople.

Mahomet IV encouraged his troops by his countenance in the camp, and beguiled the tedium of winter quarters by his favourite pastime of hunting. The sport was carried on upon a gigantic scale with thirty thousand beaters, many of whom perished by exhaustion. *"No doubt they have spoken ill of me, and God hath dealt them their reward"* was the reasonable conjecture of the Sultan upon their fate. This mighty hunter, however, relieved his army of his presence when the spring of 1683 saw it finally set in motion for the Danube. Kara Mustapha was invested with complete command. Accounts vary as to the precise point where Mahomet left his army. The ambition of his Vizier perhaps was interested ill removing so soon as possible from the field the Sultan, to whom the glory of success would have been necessarily ascribed.

Similar motives had, according to M. de la Guillatiere, caused others before this to keep the easily persuaded prince back from the camp, whither his first impulse would have led him. Oriental exaggeration is prone to magnify the hosts which Asiatic despots can command for their service. The muster-roll, found in the tent of the Grand Vizier after his defeat, affords a better basis for calculation. We find there, in round numbers, 275,000 fighting men enumerated, as the original strength of the Turkish army. Judging by the analogy of our Indian armies, the attendants and camp followers of all descriptions must have doubled these numbers.

In Hungary, the Vizier effected a junction with Count Tekeli, who was at the head of nearly 60,000 men-Hungarians, Transylvanians, Turks and Tartars. Even French officers and engineers were to be found in

□The Winged Hussars of Poland typical weapons were the saber szabla (foreground the belt 1) and the long spear kopia (2 and 3). The Great Standard Bearer of the Crown of Poland (pl. Chorazy Wielki Koronny) leads a rapier koncerz under the seat, in addition to the saber. Both riders have a pair of pistols fastened to the pommels. The wings, distinctive of the husaria, are secured to the back of the armor from the appropriate pins

Tekeli's ranks; and the character of his cause was ,indicated by coins which he caused to be struck with the inscription, *Pro Deo et Patria*. Half a million of men probably, of all creeds and races that lie between the Carpathian mountains and the Arabian deserts, were arrayed under the standard of the Prophet in the valley of the Danube. Again, according to the Turkish returns, of these 50,000 men perished in the operations before the decisive battle that relieved Vienna.

Of the whole vast multitude not more than 50,000 it was computed, ultimately regained the Turkish frontier. But even if drawn up with the best intentions, the accuracy of such returns and estimates can never be more than an approximation to the truth. It is sufficient that hundreds of thousands were marshalled beneath the Crescent to burst in a storm of desolating war upon the Christian lands.

For the struggle between Turk and Christian was not of the character of those operations to which the term of civilized warfare is conventionally applied. Prisoners were seldom made.

The Christian slaughtered; the Turk, if he spared, sold into slavery his captives; prisoners we cannot call them to whom future release was denied. Far and wide before the Turkish armies, the Tartars and the irregular horsemen, whose sole pay was plunder, whose diversion and whose business at once was rapine, spread in a desolating cloud over the country.

The whole of the unconquered Hungary, the Austrian duchy, the plains of Moravia and the mountains of Styria were swept or threatened by the scourge. Poland they had long held to be their licensed field of plunder, and now Bavaria, and Bohemia even, trembled at the terror of their approach.

The painful curiosity of their friends has attempted an estimate of the numbers of Turkish captives taken in this invasion. 32,000 grown persons, the great majority women, 204 of whom were maiden daughters of the nobility; 26,000 little children were, they tell us, carried off into slavery.

This return seems to make no mention of lads, nor of elder girls, who would perhaps form the majority of those spared for the slave-market. How many of these perished under their hardships ~ or by the Turkish disasters; how many others tasted death, but before slavery; how many others may have lost home, wealth and honour, must remain beyond enumeration or even conjecture. It is said that in lower Austria and on the frontiers of Hungary alone, 4936 villages and hamlets were given to the flames in 1683. To meet this torrent of devastation, the Emperor Leopold could muster but scanty forces.

A full half of the territory now united under the Austro-Hungarian monarchy was in the hands of the Turks, or of the Hungarian rebels; or then formed part of the territories of Poland.

The finances of Vienna have never been a source of strength. *"Business men laugh at our finance, for my part I weep over it"* said Eugene to the Emperor not long afterwards, lamenting the want of the sinews of war. The Imperial influence of Leopold in Germany was small.

The German princes were distant, jealous, slow to move. Brandenburg was irritated over the Silesian claims, that fruitful source of future war. France was all but openly hostile.

Spain was powerless. Venice, a shadow of her former self. Poland alone, under her heroic monarch, John Sobieski, might give present and substantial assistance. Yet all knew that to lean upon the support of Poland was to risk leaning upon a bruised reed indeed. Poland was, indeed, to all appearance, still a great country.

The Russian province of Poland, Lithuania, Gallicia, Posen, part of Prussia propel', were Polish. Roughly speaking, her frontiers stretched from the Dneiper to near the Oder, from the Baltic to the Carpathians. But a great territory does not make a great nation. The approaching fall of Poland was foreshadowed by her fortunes, even in the seventeenth century.

The extraordinary calamities of that country should not blind us to the means by which she brought some of her misfortunes upon her own head. Her constitution seemed skilfully contrived to unite the vices of aristocratic and democratic governments with the virtues of neither.

Her people *"Were turbulent"* without freedom, proud without steadiness of purpose. She lacked the quality and the popular support proper to a republic, as she lacked the fixed succession to the highest office and the consistent policy which are supposed to be the advantages of monarchy.

A mob of tens of thousands of armed citizens pretended to form a deliberative diet. Their convention was always a signal for confusion; their dissolution was often the prelude to civil war.

In the huge concourse a single 'Veto' could stay proceedings, unless indeed the malcontent paid for his opposition with his life. An attempt to introduce representative assemblies was always resented, and the experiment restricted, by the jealousy of the citizens. Delegates, not representatives, came to the meetings. They were vigilantly observed, and strictly cross-examined on their return, by self-constituted judges, as to the performance of their mandate. Real debate and deliberation, free judgment and rational decision, were as impossible in one kind of assembly as in the other. Below these citizen-nobles, the people were slaves. The two halves of the state, Poland and Lithuania, were set against each other continually. The monarchy became purely elective in the sixteenth century. The king was the nominee of some foreign court, or of some domestic party, or family. Factions nourished from abroad were thus kept alive.

Once elected the king found his power curtailed on every side; and was generally as solicitous for the advancement, and future succession perhaps, of his family, as for the good of the state.

He might be a stranger, or he might owe his position to the support of a foreign power. He seldom or never could be more than the nominee of some faction, the king of a party to the end of his days.

John Sobieski, the Polish king, and himself once a Polish nobleman, was not a candidate put forward by France for the Polish crown, but was generally supposed to lean towards a French connexion. His wife was French; he had passed some of his earlier years in France, and had served in Louis' musketeers of the Guard. His most formidable rival for the crown had been Charles Leopold of Lorraine,[4] the Austrian candidate, who *"Was now commanding the Imperial armies"*.

An ill omen for any unity of action in the future, between the two, against the Turks.

Sobieski had fought his way to royalty. He had contended against the enemies, from Sweden to Turkey, with whom Poland was continually embroiled. His medals bore the proud device of a sword piercing three laurel crowns, with on its point a royal diadem, and the truthful motto below, Per has ad istam.

Poland had been afflicted by Cossack insurrection, Tartar devastation and Turkish conquest. The king, Michael, had signed the disgraceful peace of Buksacs, by which the Poles became Turkish tributaries.

Sobieski and the other nobles repudiated the treaty; and at Choczim, in 1673, Sobieski overthrew the Turks with such slaughter that *"the turbans were floating thick as autumnal leaves upon the Dneister."*

The crown of Poland rewarded his victory; but the turbulence and inconstancy of his subjects prevented his reaping the fruits of success. At the most critical moments he was left destitute of men and of money, in the face of a host of Turks and Tartars. At Lemberg before his coronation, and at Zurawna after it, he was glad to have successfully defended the remainder of his country. The peace named from the latter town, left part of the Ukraine and nearly all Podolia with the fortress of Kaminiec, in Turkish hands.

The Turks scrupulously observing their part of the agreement, believed that they thereby secured the neutrality of Poland. Sobieski had suffered injuries and affronts at the hands of Austria. The punctilious pride of the Emperor was likely to add to the difficulty of forgetting these. At the last moment only would Leopold consent to address the man who was to save his empire by the title of Majesty.

The Poles either were loth to begin a new Turkish war at all, or represented the advantage which might be gained by holding aloof, till both combatants were exhausted. If they fought, Podolia, not Hungary, the recovery of Kaminiec in the former, not the relief of Vienna, should be their object.

The Lithuanians were specially jealous of Sobieski, and slow to move. The Cossacks were not to be depended upon. The country ,was exhausted of men and money by former campaigns. The French ambassador, Forbin, Cardinal de Janson, was instructed to work upon the king by promises of the future support of Louis, of visionary crowns in Hungary, and of lands in Silesia as the price of his inactivity.

No means were to be spared to detach Poland from Austria. The Cardinal worked cautiously, being an old friend and in expectation of future favours from Sobieski; but a special agent who was with him, the Marquis de Vitry, spared no pains to foment jealousies and to excite fears, and distributed money among the partisans of a peace policy. An abortive scheme was entertained for supplanting the king himself by another, more amenable to French influence. But the conspiracy was discovered, and the effect was disastrous to the French faction. The Poles rallied round the victor of Choczim and of Lemberg, and the authors of the intrigue against him were thrown into prison, or left the country.

The French agent, Vitry, himself retired from Poland. Fortunately also for Christendom, and for the house of Austria, the wife of Sobieski, Marie Casimire de la Grange d'Arquien, a Frenchwoman, had determined to

---

4 - The Duke of Lorraine had married the Emperor's sister, the widow of the late Polish king, Michael. The French had driven him from his hereditary states, and he found employment at the head of his brother in-law's armies, against them and the Turks.

thwart the diplomacy of her native land.

The failure of an intrigue, by which her father, a needy Marquis, was to have been converted into a wealthy Duke; a refusal of the French comt to receive he, a French subject by birth, as an equal should she revisit France; these causes made her an Austrian partisan. Sobieski, at the age of fifty-three, still burned with youthful ardour for his wife of forty-one, though scandal would have it that this King Arthur had his Lancelot in the Field-Marshal Jablonowski, one of the foremost of his officers. *"His incomparable Maria"* as the king addressed his queen in his frequent letters, was at all events vain and intriguing, and seldom influenced for good the husband whom she also adored.

Yet on this occasion her persuasions seconded the arguments which would undoubtedly have swayed Sobieski apart from her. His true atmosphere was that of the battle-field.

His most glorious victories were won over the infidels. The danger which menaced Austria was a common menace to Christendom. Warsaw itself would not be safe if Vienna fell. The foremost champion of the Cross would not be wanting in such a crisis. In his enthusiasm he deemed it possible to unite the jarring elements of European society in a grand crusade. Visions floated before him of a great League, including the Christian powers and the Persians, by which the Turkish Empire should be overthrown, Constantinople recovered, Moldavia and Wallachia united to the Polish crown, and a republic of Athens and the Morea established.

A scheme too great for accomplishment in the face of the selfishness of France and Austria and the inherent weakness of Poland. But a general subscription was needed to put any army into the field at all.

Rome and Italy were foremost in contributions; even ecclesiastical property was allowed to be mortgaged in the cause.

The Pope, an economical reformer in Rome, as befitted the member of a banking family, the Odescalchi, was able to provide two million scudi. Christina, ex-Queen of Sweden, bestirred herself to increase the fund. The Regent of Portugal sent money, and sanctified the gift by a simultaneous holocaust of Jews.

1,200,000 florins were to be advanced by the Emperor to pay the Polish troops. The Pope undertook to guarantee the repayment, and contributions were expected from the King of Spain. Both these latter alike were swayed by the double motive-fear of the Turks, and the desire to set free the Empire to act against France again. Leopold, as his contribution to the harmony of the allies, had condescended to yield the title of *"Majesty"* to the King of Poland, and had held out hopes of a marriage between the son of Sobieski and an Austrian Archduchess, which might ensure the succession of the former to his father's throne. A dispensation from the Pope released the Poles from the duty of keeping their oaths to the Turks.

The Emperor and the King exchanged oaths not to resort to such a dispensation from then.' engagements to each other. The treaty of alliance was signed; but before the Polish troops could be mustered in any numbers, the Turkish armies had united with those of Tekeli, and were pouring across the frontier.

▲ Serhadkulu Cavalry (XVII century), Delil. Delil were the élite troop of the Ottoman border cavalry in Europe. Native of Hungary or of the Balkans, thay used weapons not unlike those supplied to the Polish-Lithuanian (2 used a lance equal to the Polish kopia), often preferring the saber or the backsword to the Turkish scimitar, and alternating to kalkan shield (3) the Hungarian shield (1 and 2).

CHAPTER IV

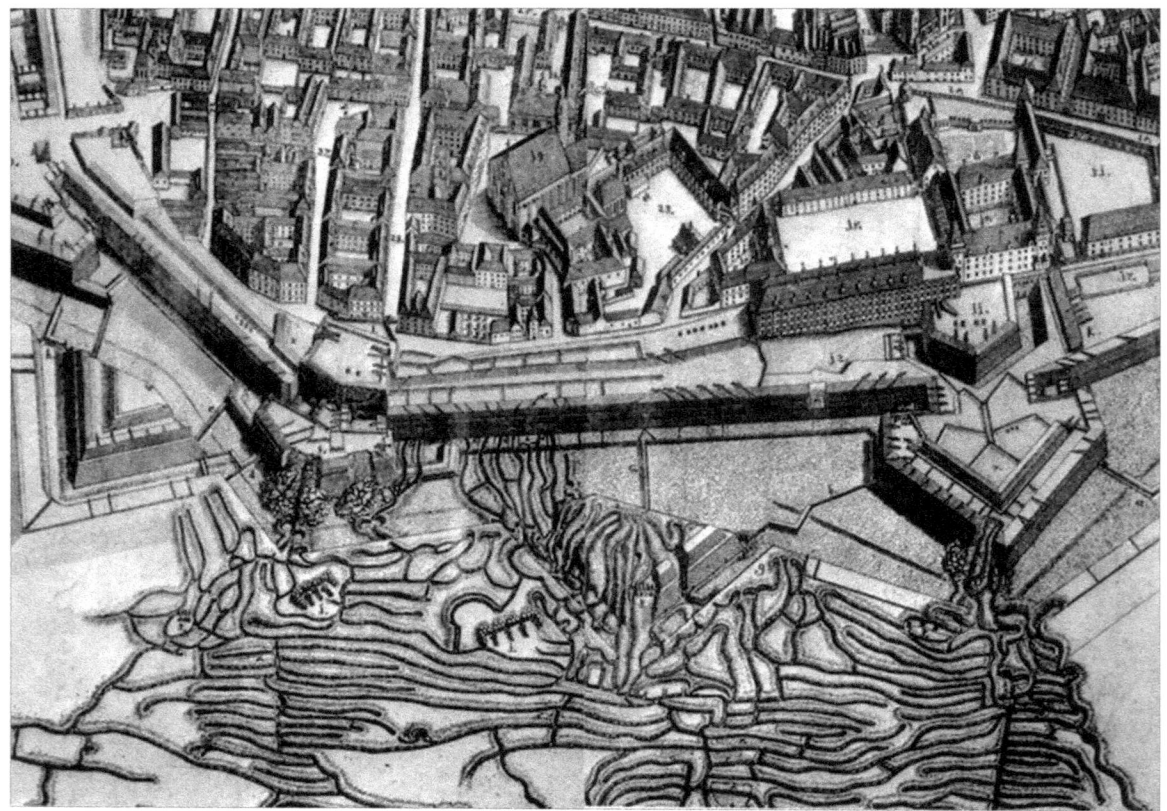

▲ The Hofburg bastion side of Veinna and the several turkish siege gallery

CHAPTER IV

Charles of Lorraine, the Imperial commander, had under his orders less than 40,000. The levy en 'masse of Hungary produced 3000 soldiers only for the Emperor's service, so wide was the sway of the Turks, or so universal the sympathy for Tekeli. Six thousand Hungarians, supposed to be raised for the Emperor, went over to the enemy as soon as they advanced. Yet, contrary to his own opinion, Lorraine began with offensive operations against the Turkish fortress of Neuhausel.

A partial success was followed by a disastrous repulse, and the army withdrew south of the Danube, as the main Turkish force approached upon that same side of the river. Lorraine had some idea of making a stand near the Raab to cover the Austrian frontier, but the number of the enemy and the temper of his own soldiers rendered such an attempt too hazardous. He determined to retreat, and await the reinforcements already promised by the Princes of the Empire. Garrisons were hastily flung into Raab, Komorn, and Leopoldstadt.

The infantry then recrossed the Danube and fell back towards Vienna along the Schutt island, under Count Leslie's orders.

The cavalry marched upon the southern side of the river, but the superior rapidity of their retreat did not save them from molestation. On July 7 at Petronel, some twenty miles below Vienna, 15,000 Spahis and Tartars burst upon their march. For a time Count Taaffe, with the rear guard of 400 men, was in extreme danger. The exertions of Lorraine and of Louis of Baden rallied the cavalry and speedily repulsed their disorderly assailants, but in the confusion several of the officers fell, including Prince Aremberg and Julius Louis of Savoy, an elder brother of Prince Eugene, and much of the baggage became the prey of the Tartars.

Altenburg and Haimburg, posts upon the Danube, had been already stormed, after a brief resistance, by the Turkish infantry. Those stragglers who first leave the field are always apt to cover their own flight by the report of an universal overthrow. So fugitives came galloping to Vienna with a tale of disaster.

They spread the rumour that the Duke of Lorraine was killed and the army totally defeated, while their alarm seemed amply confirmed by the glow of burning villages that brightened upon the twilight of the eastern horizon. The Imperial court, which had delayed its flight so far, in the hope that the enemy might linger about the fortresses of Raab or of Komorn, tarried now no longer. *"Leopold could never bear to hear plain truths but when he was afraid"* says Eugene. He had refused to recognize the imminence of the peril until now; and by his confidence had involved in his destruction others, who had not the same means of escape at the last moment which he himself possessed. Yet means of escape were barely open to him, when at length he understood that he must defend or abandon his capital.

The roads to Upper Austria and to Bavaria, along the southern shore of the Danube, were rightly distrusted. The Emperor, his Empress, and the Empress Mother, with all their train of courtiel's, of ladies, and of servants, shorn of pomp and bereft of dignity in their flight, poured over the Leopoldstadt island and the Tabor bridge in all the misery of panic fear.

The prompt destruction of the bridge of Crems, above Vienna, is said alone to have saved their route from interception by the Tartars. A part of their baggage actually became the prey of the marauders.

The whole court, including even the Empress herself, who was far advanced in pregnancy, were driven to seek rest in farms and cottages.

Once they passed the night under a temporary shelter of boughs. In the universal panic, small room was left for hopes of a return to the capital and to the palaces that they had quitted. Milan, Innsbruck, Prague were thought of as their future refuge. On to Linz, and from Linz to the frontier they fled, till their confidence at last returned behind the fortifications of the Bavarian city of Passau. But they were not the only fugitives from Vienna. The bold march of the Vizier upon the city, leaving Raab, Komorn, and Presburg in his rear, to fall an easy prey when once the great prize was captured; this had taken the citizens by surprise.

The retreat of Lorraine, and the skirmish at Petronel, had filled them with abject terror. People from the surrounding country who had taken shelter in Vienna no longer relied upon her as a stronghold, but turned their thoughts to an escape to Bavaria, or to Styria, or even to the distant Tirol. From nine o'clock in the evening till two o'clock in the morning, on the 7th and 8th of July, a never-ending stream of carriages and of fugitives were following in the track of the Imperial cortege. East and south, upon the horizon, the glare of burning villages told that the Turkish horsemen were there. High on the summit of the Kahlenberg, the flames of the Camalduline Convent dreadfully illuminated the track of the fugitives. Sixty thousand persons, it was believed, left the city in the course of a few days. Of those who, crossing the Danube, took the roads into Upper Austria or into Moravia, some fell into the hands of the Hungarian and Tartar marauders. But few of those who attempted to escape into Styria succeeded in reaching a place of safety.

They perished by thousands, enveloped by the flying squadrons of the invaders. In Vienna herself, deserted by her leaders and by so many of her children, violent tumult raged against the Government, and against the Jesuits, who were supposed to have instigated the persecution of the Protestants of Hungary.

There was ample cause for terror. The fortifications were old and imperfect, the suburbs encroached upon the works, the number of the defenders was small. Thirteen thousand infantry, supplied by the army of Lorraine, and seven thousand armed citizens formed the garrison; and, besides these, about sixty thousand souls were in the city. The command was entrusted to Ernest Rudiger Count Starhemberg, an officer of tried skill and courage. He had served with Montecuccoli against the Turks, and against both Condé and Turenne with the same commander and with the Prince of Orange.

He entered the city as the fugitives forsook it. He set the people to work upon the fortifications, organized them for defence, and assured them that he would live and die with them. But while writing to the Emperor that he would joyfully spend the last drop of his blood in defence of his charge, he confesses that the place is in want of everything, and the inhabitants panic-stricken.

Fortunately he and others with him were the class of men to restore confidence in the rest. Under him served many noble volunteers, for the example of the Emperor was not universally followed. The Bishop of Neustadt, once himself a soldier and a knight of Malta, was conspicuous among many brave and devoted men for his liberal donations to the troops, and for his superintendence of the sanitary state of the city. In one respect alone the place was well furnished; three hundred and twenty-one pieces of artillery were supplied by the Imperial arsenal for the fortifications.[5]

The city was defended after the existing fashion, with ten bastions, the curtains covered by ravelines, with a ditch mostly dry. On the side of the Danube was merely a wall with towers and platforms, and all the works were more or less uncared for and decayed. The work of fixing palisades was postponed till the Turkish army was in sight. It is possible that by a slightly more rapid march the Vizier might have secured Vienna by a coup de main. On July 13, the Turkish regular cavalry came in sight, preceding the infantry of the main army; and at the last possible moment fire was set to the suburbs, which impeded the defence.

A high wind speedily caused them to be consumed. On the 14th, the Turkish army took up its position, encamping in a semicircle, round the whole of the circuit of the defences not washed by the Danube.

A city, surpassing in size and population the beleaguered capital, sprang up about the walls of Vienna.

The tents of the Vizier were pitched opposite the Burg bastion, in the suburb of St. Ulric. The camp was crowded not only by soldiers, but by the merchants of the East, who thronged thither as to a fail to deal in the plunder of the Christians.

The Imperial troops still attempted to hold the Leopoldstadt island; but on July 16, the Turks threw bridges across the arm of the Danube, and shortly drove the Christians to the northern bank of the river. The houses of the Leopoldstadt were given up to fire by the Turks; and the bridge, leading to the northern shore, destroyed by the Imperialists. The investment of Vienna was now completed upon every side. Batteries from the Leopoldstadt, and from the south and west, crossed it with fire in all directions. Trenches were opened, and the elaborate approaches and frequent mines of the Turks, advancing with alarming rapidity, enveloped the western and south-western face of the works from the Scottish gate to the Burg bastion.

---

5 Together with forty two guns and eight howitzers from the city arsenal. Among the Emperor's pieces were eleven gigantic mortars, described as 100,150, and 200 pounders, but two hundred and fifty three of the guns were smaller than 12 pounders.

Upwards of three hundred pieces of artillery played upon the crumbling defences and the devastated city. The pavement of the streets was tom up, that the balls might bury themselves in the soft earth where they fell. The upper floors and roofs of the houses were barricaded with heavy timber, or covered with sandbags, to guard against the fire of the dropping shells. The streets themselves were blocked behind the walls, chains drawn across them, and the houses loop-holed and prepared for defence to the last extremity.

All the gates had been walled up but one, the Stuben gate, which, being partially covered by the stream of the Wien, was left open as a sally-port. Early in the siege, the assailed, frequently issuing forth, returned the attacks of the enemy, frustrated their operations, and even captured provisions in the hostile lines.

But as time went on, the diminishing numbers of the garrison forbade the waste of life incurred even in successful sorties.

The progress of the Turks was rapid with sap and mine. They were famed for their skill with entrenching and engineering tools, and the Christians learnt much from them, though their approaches were unlike the ordinary European works. Instead of parallel lines to the defences they drew curves, overlapping each other and continually approaching the place attacked. The trenches were deep, and fifteen or sixteen feet wide at the bottom where the ground allowed. The depth of the Turkish works effectually protected their soldiers, even when they had made a lodgement in the ditch; for the besieged could not depress their cannon sufficiently to hurt them. They were protected skilfully by bomb-proof shelters of timber and of turf, beneath which thousands of men, hidden and shielded, crouched ready for attack, or for the repulse of sorties.

Their mines penetrated in every direction to the counterscarp of the place, and ultimately to the walls themselves. At length the very cellars of the nearest houses were threatened by a subterranean enemy; and water and drums strewn with peas were placed in them, to tell, by the slightest vibration, of the work of the Turkish miner's pick below. The Turkish miners were bolder than those of the garrison.

The latter were hired labourers of the lowest class, of whom Starhemberg wrote to Lorraine that nothing would induce them to re-enter a mine after they had heard the sound of the enemy working near them.

On the part of the enemy, men who had applied for a Timar, or military fief, often volunteered as miners to prove their courage and to win its reward. At the very beginning of operations the city ail but perished through a fire, which actually reached the windows of the Imperial arsenal stored with eighteen hundred barrels of powder. An explosion there would have opened a road for the Turkish army into Vienna, at once deprived of the means of resistance and reduced to ruins.

The exertions of Captain Count Guido Starhemberg, nephew of the commandant, who personally superintended the removal of the powder through the opposite windows, together with a lucky change of wind, saved the city. Rightly or wrongly, an incendiary was suspected. The fear of treachery was added to the legitimate terrors of the citizens. Desertions took place to the enemy, and spies were actually apprehended within the wails. Hungarians and other Christians were arrayed upon both sides, and this community of language and manners, between besiegers and besieged, rendered such a danger more real.

But from the open force of the attack the worst calamities were to be feared. On the 23rd, 25th, and 27th of July the opening assaults were delivered. All were repulsed, but with loss of lives ill-spared.

Closer and closer crept the Turkish sappers. Assault after assault upon the outer fortifications gradually wrested important positions from the besieged. The Burg and Lowel bastions, with the connecting curtain between them and the Burg ravel in, were reduced to an almost shapeless ruin by the Turkish mines and artillery. Every device was tried to retard the attack. The arts and ingenuity of a great city were at the service of the besieged. They made their own powder; and, when hand-grenades began to fail, the invention of an officer supplied their place with grenades of earthenware. Nevertheless, on August 7, the Turks made a lodgement upon the counterscarp, after twenty-three days of firing and terrible losses upon both sides.

The Janissaries now stood upon the very threshold of the city. Hand to hand fighting was carried on in the ditches. The citizens armed with scythes upon the end of poles contended with advantage from above against the Turkish sabres. Boiling pitch and water stood continually ready to overwhelm the assailants as they struggled up the shattered slope of the ramparts. Besiegers and besieged were continually within pistol shot of each other, and showers of Turkish arrows descended on the town. As yet no footing was obtained by the Turks within the body of the place, though the streets and houses stood ready barricaded against such an event. But the Vizier commanded two hundred thousand men, Starhemberg but twenty thousand. Disease

▲ Istanbul-Costantinople the Ottoman capital.

and the toils and losses of the defence told fearfully upon the latter. Starhemberg himself was disabled by dysentery early in the siege, and did all that man could do, carried in a chair from post to post, amidst the hottest of the fire. On the other side, Kara Mustapha made his rounds in a litter rendered shot-proof by plates of iron. The chief engineer of the garrison, Rimpler, fell. Colonel Barner, commanding the artillery, and the Prince of Wurttemberg were disabled. Five thousand men, more than a third of the regular soldiers, perished. Food became scarce, vermin were eagerly sought for by the poor, and dysentery followed inevitably ill the train of want. Fever sprang from the confinement, filth, and bad air inseparable from their condition.

Sixty persons a day were dying of dysentery alone towards the conclusion of the siege. But the humour of the Viennese asserted itself still among their calamities, and the spoils of nocturnal chase upon the tiles were sold as *"Roof Hares"* in the market. The courage of long endurance, that rarest of all courage, was tried to the uttermost. The Bishop of Neustadt, bravest of the brave defenders, laboured unremittingly among the sick, nor cared less for the safety of the whole, by undertaking the control of sanitary measures.

The otherwise useless non combatants were organized by him into bands of scavengers, hospital attendants, and carriers of the wounded.

A despatch from Starhemberg, dated August 18, came safely to the hands of Lorraine. The commandant wrote boldly, perhaps with an eye to the probability of his intelligence reaching the Turkish and not the Imperial general. I must in the first place, tell your Highness that we have up to this moment disputed the works with the enemy, foot by foot, and that they have not gained an inch of ground without paying for it dearly.

Every time that, sword in hand, they have attempted a lodgement, they have been vigorously repulsed by our men, with such loss that they no longer dare to put their heads out of their holes.*"Nevertheless, he was providing for the worst."* I have caused a new work, well ditched, to be made in the middle of the Burg ravelin; the Lowel and Burg bastions are also defended by a second line; and I am even now beginning another work behind these same bastions. I write this that your Highness may know that we are forgetting nothing, that we are wide awake, and taking all imaginable precautions. As in duty bound I assure your Highness, that to show myself worthy of the confidence which your Highness, and more especially his Majesty my master, repose in my small services, I shall never yield the place but with the last drop of my blood.

This despatch was safely carried to Lorraine by Kolschitzki, a Pole. Many other letters had miscarried, for few messengers penetrated, at the risk of life, between the city and the slowly mustering forces of Lorraine. Some swam the arms of the Danube. The most skilful, however, was this Kolschitzki, who relied upon his knowledge of the Turkish tongue and manners, and in Turkish dress penetrated the besieging lines, much as a countryman of our own relied on similar knowledge in a scarcely less memorable siege.

The name of Kolschitzki of Vienna may be named side by side with that of *"Lucknow"* Kavanagh, though the Pole not only passed out through the besiegers, but succeeded in returning again in a like manner into the city with despatches, to sustain the courage of the defenders. From his stone chair, high up in the fretted spire of St. Stephen's, the watchman saw the rockets which rose as signals from the Christian outposts north of the Danube. But from the southern bank must the march be made for the deliverance of the city; and was it possible that Lorraine, or even Sobieski, could carry a force across the river in the face of such an army? The garrison record, with painful exactness, the terrible annals of the siege; what ravelin is deluged with the blood of assailants and of defenders; where mines have blown the counterscarp into the ditch, or shattered the salient angle of a bastion; what new quarter of the city is devastated by the cannonade; what much-prized life is taken; when the bread begins to fail; what false hopes of relief, or what exaggerated tidings of calamity, circulate among the citizens.

These details, of overwhelming interest to every man at the moment, and printed indelibly upon his mind, bring to the distant observer but one confused and appalling panorama of suffering and of endurance, of courage and of despair.

The growing anxiety of the city appears in a second despatch of Starhemberg's, dated August 27.

He still tells of attacks repulsed, of sorties boldly executed, and of mines discovered and foiled, but he acknowledges the need of succour. We are losing many men and many officers, more from dysentery than from the enemy's fire, the deaths from that disease alone are sixty daily. We have no more grenades, which were our best defence; our guns are some of them destroyed by the enemy's fire, some of them burst before firing fifty rounds, from the bad material used by the founder; and the enemy, seeing they can hold their lodgements in the ditch with a few men, are massing great numbers on the counterscarp, to have a large force ready there for some extraordinary effort .... ,We await, therefore, your Highness's arrival with extreme impatience; for my own part not so much from a wish to be relieved as that I may have the honour of respectfully assuring your Highness of my obedience, being, as I am, your Highness's most humble and obedient servant, Starhemberg. The courtly bravado of the subscription is in strong contrast with the hurried postscript that follows:*"My miners tell me that they hear the enemy working beneath them under the Burg bastion; they must have run their gallery from the other side of the ditch, and there is no time to be lost."*

When this despatch was written, both sides believed that the supreme crisis was at hand. The 29th of August was looked for as the decisive day. On that anniversary Stuhlweissenberg and Belgrade had fallen before the Ottomans. Above all, on that day the strength of Hungary had been smitten, and her king, Louis, had died, before the hosts of the great Solyman, on the disastrous field of "The Destruction of Mohacs"- that battle which first opened Hungary and Austria to the invader. But the 29th came and passed, with no general attack from the besiegers. A mine was sprung under the Burg ravelin, nearly completing the ruin of the work; and three or four hundred Turks attempted to establish themselves upon the remains, but were driven back again. Another mine was sprung by the Burg bastion, but no assault followed. From St. Stephen's considerable movement was noticed among the Turkish detachments on the left bank of the Danube, occasioned by the march of Lorraine's army. In the camp murmurs and dissensions ran high.

The Janissaries clamoured at their lengthy detention in the trenches. They openly accused the incapacity, or worse faults, of the Vizier. There seems little doubt but that he had it in his power to have overwhelmed the defenders by a general and prolonged assault, towards the end of August. Ottoman leaders had known well how to avail themselves of the obedience and fatalist courage of their soldiers. Ammath IV, when he won back Baghdad from the Persians, Mahomet II, at the taking of Constantinople, had shown how cities could be won. Before the city of the Khalifs for three days, before the city of the Caesars from a May sunrise till well nigh noon, had torrent after torrent of brave, devoted, undisciplined soldiers wearied the arms and exhausted the ammunition of the defenders, until the Janissaries arose, fresh and invincible for the decisive charge.

▲ The Turkish commander and his jannissaries.

Wave after wave of stormers, fed from inexhaustible multitudes, had rolled upon the besieged, and, like broken waves, had rolled back in ruin, until the last and greatest should burst in overwhelming force upon the breaches. Such an assault would have been surely successful against Vienna.

But the Vizier, in vain security, pictured to himself the advantages of a surrender, which should preserve the city as a trophy of his conquest- the seat, perchance, of his sovereignty. The riches which he dreamed it to contain, he hoped to receive as his own spoil; not to yield as the booty of the army after a storm.

So, while the decisive days passed, the signal for attack was delayed, except by small bodies upon single points, until the courage of his soldiers was dissipated and their confidence destroyed.

On the contrary, the unexpected reprieve gave courage to the defenders. The Janissaries, on the other hand, impatiently invoked the appearance of the relieving army to end their sojourn in the trenches by the decisive event of a stricken field. Slowly, but at last, ere yet too late, that army was approaching.

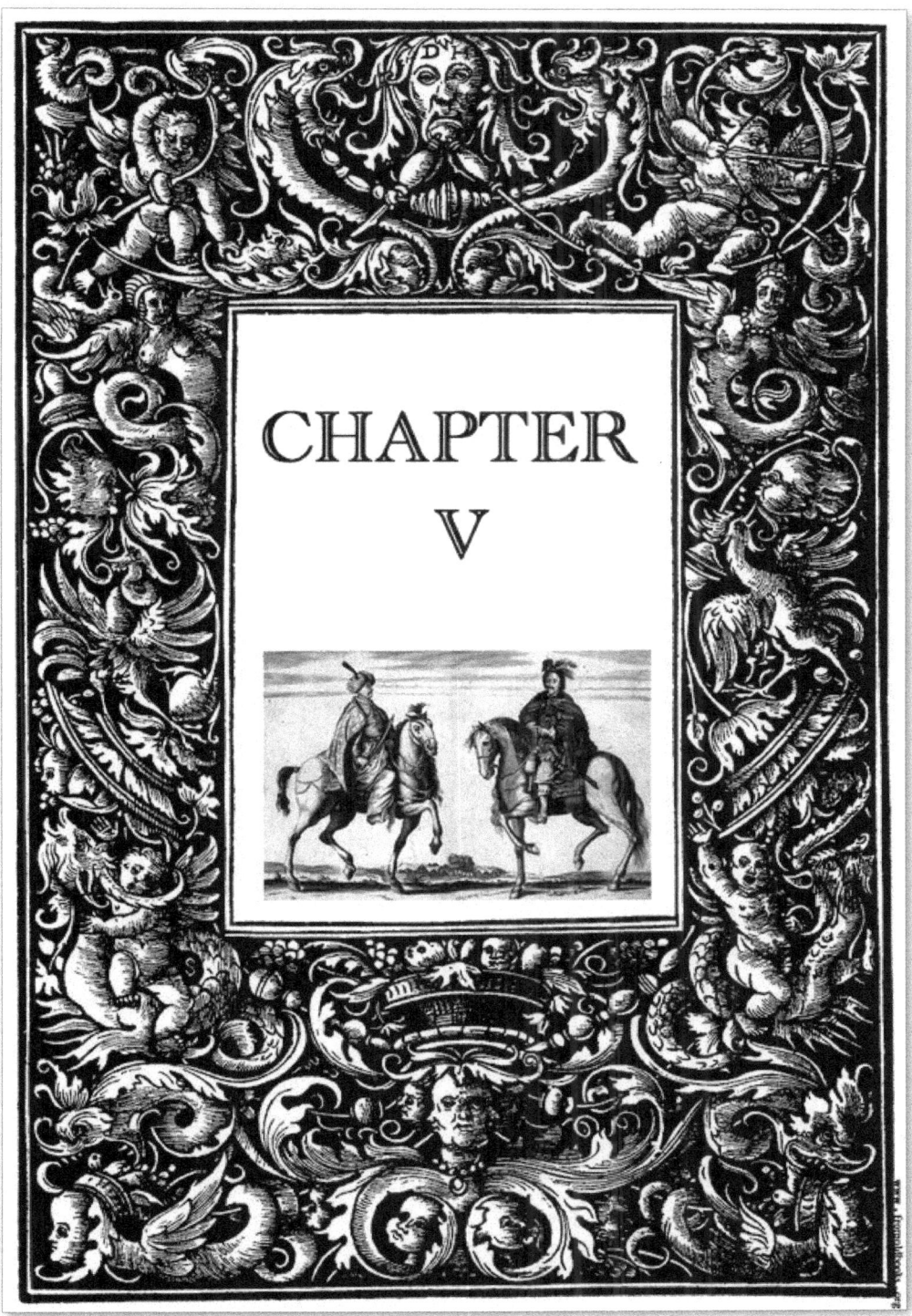

CHAPTER
V

▲ Jannissaires infantrymen of the Yaya Ortasi with a parade dolama caftan and the ak bork headgear distinctive of the body. Oglan, recruits janissary enlisted with the devsirme system, wearing a conical hat and dolama.

CHAPTER V

The duties which had been imposed upon Charles of Lorraine were of the most arduous kind. With a handful of troops, but slowly reinforced by the German levies, whose assistance was rendered less useful by the jealousies of the sovereign Princes in command, he was opposed both to the Turks and to Tekeli. He was expected to be ready to support the garrisons of Presburg and of Komorn, to hinder the incursions of the enemy into Upper Austria and into Moravia-above all, to prepare the bridges above Vienna, by which alone a relieving army could arrive. Though driven from the Leopoldstadt island, and from all immediate communication with the city, his presence yet animated the besieged with hope of succour. He fixed his head-quarters finally at Krems, on the Danube, where the Saxon contingent presently arrived, followed by the troops of the Circles and the Bavarians.

Before their arrival, towards the end of August, he felt strong enough to advance and rescue Presburg from Tekeli. He followed up the operation by a defeat inflicted on the combined forces of the Turks and Hungarians upon the Marchfeld. A detachment of four thousand Polish horse, under Lubomirski, originally raised to assist Tekeli, were already present with the army of Lorraine.

But decisive operations were of necessity postponed till after the coming of the King of Poland with the bulk of his forces, and of the rest of the German troops. Lorraine, in these movements, undoubtedly proved his title to generalship; but nothing except the extraordinary apathy of the Vizier rendered them possible.

A skilful employment of the enormous force of Turkish cavalry must have forced the Imperial army to retire for want of supplies. The ravage, aimlessly and mercilessly inflicted upon Austria and the confines of Moravia, would, if directed against Poland, have probably prevented the march of Sobieski.

An able commander, with such forces at his command, might have prevented, or at least hindered, the junction of the Poles and Germans. Nor were any steps taken by the Vizier to stop the construction of the bridges at Krems and at Tuln, nor to guard the defiles of the Wiener Wald, over which the Christian army must advance to raise the siege. So extraordinary indeed was the neglect of the enemy, that a secret understanding has been supposed between Tekeli and Sobieski, by which, in return for the future good offices of the latter, the former was not to molest Poland nor hinder the junction of the Christian forces.

Be that as it may, the secret information of the Poles was as good as that of the Turks was bad, and the king knew thoroughly with what foes he had to deal. Meanwhile, in spite of French intrigues, in spite of backwardness in Lithuania and of distrust in Poland, Sobieski had left Warsaw for Cracow on July 18. Up to the last moment the Turks disbelieved in his coming in person, and the Emperor and the French king both doubted it.

He was gouty, he was rheumatic, he was too fat to ride; such was the tenour of the information of the baffled French agent Vitry. Nevertheless, on the 22nd of August, he was on the Silesian frontier with the main part of his army. It consisted mostly of cavalry, of those Polish horsemen matchless in prowess, but the most unstable of forces. His infantry was less numerous and inferior, their shabby accoutrements contrasting sharply with the gaudy equipment of the cavaliers. *"They have sworn to dress themselves better in the spoils of the enemy"* said the king of one regiment, deprecating the criticism of the Germans.

His march lay through Silesia and Moravia, through the borders of the lands devastated by the Tartars, where the trembling inhabitants thronged around him, hailing him already as their deliverer. Urged by message after message from Lorraine, he left his army to follow under the leadership of the Field Marshal Jablonowski, and hurried on himself at the head of two thousand cavalry, his son Prince James by his side. We can follow every movement of the campaign from the letters which, amid the hurry of the march, during short hours snatched from sleep, once at least during the thunder of a Turkish cannonade, he found time to despatch continually to his queen. *Seule joie de mon ame, charmante et bien-aimée Mariette*, as he calls her. Her letters in reply are his continual consolation amid the labours of the campaign, the ingratitude of the Emperor, and the insubordination of his subjects. *"I read all your letters, my dear and incomparable Maria, thrice over-once when I receive them, once when I retire to my tent and am alone with my love, once when I sit down to answer them."* Such is his answer to her expression of a fear that the distractions of his enterprise

▲ The battle under the Vienna' walls in a contemporary engraving.

may leave no time for interest in aught besides. On August 29 he writes, from near Brunn in Moravia, sending the news of the retreat of Tekeli after his defeat by Lorraine, and adding that he hopes the next day, on nearing the Danube, to hear the cannon which tell that Vienna is still untaken.

On the 31st he is near Tuln, above Vienna. He has passed the distant thunder of the cannonade upon his left hand, and has effected his junction with the army of Lorraine. Despairing of the arrival of the Lithuanians, he has distributed the arms intended for them among the imperfectly equipped Poles.

Still more is he distressed at the non-appearance of the Cossacks, whom he expected, and whom he knew as invaluable for outpost duty. Menzynski, who should have conducted them, is lingering at Lemberg. *"C'est un grand miserable."* Most interesting of all is the passage in which he gives his wife his first impressions of his future colleague, the Duke of Lorraine. Lorraine had been a competitor with Sobieski for the crown of Poland, and it must have been a singular meeting when the rivals first came face to face co-operating together in a mighty enterprise. Sobieski the king, whose offspring were not to reign; Charles the duke, the destined ancestor of the Imperial line of Austria.[6]

The one in the semi-Oriental magnificence of his country, he went into action before Vienna in a sky-blue silk doublet; the other in the dress of a campaigner, best described in Sobieski's own words. The duke he

6 - The grandson of the Duke of Lorraine married Maria Theresa, Queen of Hungary, and was himself Emperor. The grand daughter of Sobieski was the mother of Charles Edward, the hero of the Forty-five.

finds modest and taciturn, stooping, plain, with a hooked nose, marked with small-pox; clad in an old grey coat, with *"a fair wig ill-made, a hat without a band "* boots of yellow leather, or rather of what was yellow three months ago.*"Avec tout ca, il n'a pas la mine d'un marchand, mais d'un homme comme il faut, et meme d'un homme de distinction. C'est un homme avec qui je m'accorderais facilement. "* The friendship of the former rivals was cemented by a banquet, and the duke's accustomed monitor being first overcome, Lorraine himself was induced to proceed from his native Moselle, which he drank usually mixed with water, to the strong Hungarian wines-to the improvement, as the king tells his wife, of his conversation.

Besides Lorraine, Sobieski found a crowd of German Princes awaiting his arrival: John George of Saxony, speaking no French nor Latin, and very little German; Waldeck, of the house of Waldeck-Wildungen, William the Third's right hand man in the Netherlands, here commanding the troops of the Circles, and winning high praise from the king for his activity and zeal; Maximilian of Bavaria, whose courage and ill fortune were hereafter to be signalized at Blenheim and at Ramilies, now aged twenty-one, wins notice as better dressed than the others.

There were two Wurtembergers and the Prince of Brunswick Luneburg, afterwards our George I.; the Prince of Saxe-Lauenberg; a Hohenzollern and a Hessian; three Princes of Anhalt; Hermann and Louis of Baden, the latter was with Marlborough at Schellenberg; two sons of Montecuccoli, the conqueror of St. Gotthard; last and youngest, though not least, Eugene of Savoy, the future conqueror of Zenta and of Belgrade, and the colleague of Marlborough in his greatest battles.

There was Count Leslie, of that Scotch house which had given generals to half the armies of Europe; Count Taaffe, the Irishman, afterwards Sir Francis Taaffe and Earl of Carlingford, whose elder brother fell fighting for King James at the Boyne, but whose services to the allies secured the earldom from forfeiture. There were gathered veterans of the Thirty Years' War, men who might have seen Gustavus or Wallenstein, and men who were to reap their brightest laurels hereafter in the war of the Spanish Succession. As was wittily said, the Empire would have been there had only the Emperor been present.

The Brandenburg troops also were wanting. The *"Great Elector"* was jealous of Poland-once his superior in the Prussian duchy had formerly been injured by Sobieski acting with the Swedes in the interests of France, and moreover was not on the best terms with the Emperor.

Brandenburg, then as ever, was playing with skill and patience her own game. The fortunes of the future Prussian monarchy were not to be lightly risked for the sake of Austria. But the Emperor himself must not be rashly charged with want of courage for his absence from the camp. He was not trained to war; the presence of his court would have been embarrassing to the operations, perhaps would have been inseparable from intrigues and jealousies that would seriously have crippled the army.

A certain stubborn manhood Leopold had shown in not yielding to the pressure put upon him to make terms with Louis XIV in this extremity. The aid of France could have been purchased by the election of the Dauphin as King of the Romans, probably by smaller sacrifices.

The Diet at Ratisbon had been not disinclined to yield, but the Emperor had stedfastly refused to subject either his own house or the Empire to French dictation. That one crowned head was in the field was of the greatest importance, especially when that one was the King of Poland. Everywhere the most cheerful deference was rendered to Sobieski by all who were present. The Princes, jealous of each other before, now vied with each other in zealous obedience to the conqueror of Choczim. His experience of Turkish warfare was unique, his personal character commanding. He tells his wife how Lorraine, Waldeck, Saxony, Bavaria would send or even come personally for his commands.

The ascendancy exercised by Sobieski is nowhere more decisively illustrated than in the conduct of five hundred Janissaries, a trophy of his victories, who now formed his body guard. He offered them leave of absence from the battle, or even a free passage to the Turkish camp, but they besought leave to live and die with him, if The king himself was fully prepared to accept the advice of generals like Lorraine and Waldeck. He had left his royal dignity behind at Warsaw, as he told Lorraine, and at once agreed with the latter upon a plan for crossing the Danube at Krems and at Tuln, concentrating at Tuln and marching over the Kahlenberg to Vienna. He only complained of the backward condition of the bridges and of the slow assemblage of the troops, whereas the Emperor had by letter assured him that all was ready before he had left Poland. When finally assembled, the united armies numbered eighty-five thousand men.

The Poles were more than twenty-six thousand strong. But allowing for detachments, not more than seventy-seven thousand men were available upon the battlefield. The artillery numbered one hundred and sixty-eight pieces, of which few came into action.

On September 4, the king still writes from near Tuln. If an excess of glory is often the share of a successful commander, yet an excessive toil is his always. Sobieski tells his wife that he has a continual cold and headache, and is night and day in the saddle.

The French stories were so far true that he could not mount without assistance, yet in the midst of such operations no rest is possible. The Turks are, he says, either really ignorant of his presence, or refuse to believe it.

The Vizier was incredibly ill-supplied with information. He really was uncertain whether Sobieski was in the field; and whether the Polish army, or partisan corps only, like that of Lubomirski, had joined Lorraine.

The smallest resistance would seriously have retarded the passage of the Danube, performed by the Germans at Krems, by the Poles at Tuln. As it was, the difficulties were terrible. The pontoons sank under the weight of the artillery and waggons. The latter had to find fords over the smaller branches of the river, while the bridges upon the main stream were strengthened to sustain them.

Even then much baggage was left north of the Danube; much more upon the southern side, entrenched and defended. On September 8, when the concentration of the army upon the southern bank was being completed, Marco d'Aviano, the Emperor's Confessor, celebrated a solemn mass, and gave a formal benediction to the Christian army. Sobieski then stepped forward, and after addressing some words of encouragement to the assembled officers, bestowed the honour of knighthood upon his son James.[7]

An enthusiastic votary of his religion, he desired to impress upon his army that their cause was the cause of God, against the enemies of the Faith. Even the Lutheran Saxons and North Germans could, with more justice than the Hungarian renegades, claim to be fighting *Pro Deo et Patria*. Upon the coming struggle depended the question whether the frightful devastation, which had desolated Hungary and Austria, was or was not to be repeated in all the south German lands. The flat ground upon the southern side of the Danube, from near Krems to Tuln, the Tullner Feld, offered a convenient space for the mustering of the army after passing the river. Vienna was not further than about sixteen miles as the crow flies, but the intervening country was of a difficult nature, even should the Turks attempt no interruption to the movements of the relieving forces. The Wiener Wald, rising to more than nine hundred feet above the level of the Danube, runs into a north-easterly direction between Tuln and Vienna, and advances up to the very current of the river, which flows north-eastward and then south-eastward round the mountain barrier.

The roads were few and difficult, and trees covered the slopes of the hills. Sobieski had decided to advance with his left wing covered by the Danube, and to throw sucour into Vienna upon that side; while with the right he threatened the rear of the Turkish camp on the side of Dornbach and Hernals.

With this object the march was directed upon the Leopoldsberg and the Kahlenberg, the last heights or ridges of the mountains above the Danube, to the north-west of Vienna. And at length, on the 10th of September, the forward movement upon the Kahlenberg began. Already as early as the morning of the 6th, a reconnaissance had been pushed to the summit, and as evening fell had cheered Vienna with a flight of signal rockets, in answer to the fiery messengers of distress which nightly rose from the spire of St. Stephen's. But to carry an army up the Kahlenberg was a harder task. Sobieski wrote that the country was horribly wasted. There was neither food for man nor forage for horses, beyond what the army could carry with them.

Indeed, the leaves of the trees upon the Kahlenberg had to eke out the supplies of the latter. There was all need for despatch. The last despairing message had come from Starhemberg, borne by a swimmer on the Danube to Lorraine, in language as brief as significant, *"No time to be lost; no time indeed to be lost."*

---

7 - Schimmer"Sieges of Vienna;"Count Thurheim"Life of Starhemberg;"and Salvandy"Hist. de Pologne"p. 172, vol. ii. misplace this solemn benediction of the army and the knighting of Prince James on the morning of the 12th. Sobieski's own testimony, in his letters to his queen, is decisive for the 8th. Nor on the 12th was there time for the ceremony.

▲ Turkish cavalryman in the battle of Vienna.

▲ The Cossack infantryman (1) in the early XVII century still looks very "barbaric". As the Tartars, often wears coarse woolen clothes and animal fur.Most of the soldiers lacks firearms, preferring the bow, the sword or the massive bardiche poleaxe.
The few muskets available, usually tüfek stolen from Turkish-Tartars, are carried in protective covers. The Starshina officers (2), close to the Polish-Lithuanian noble clans and often related with them, have instead a costume much more similar to that of the Commonwealth's nobility.

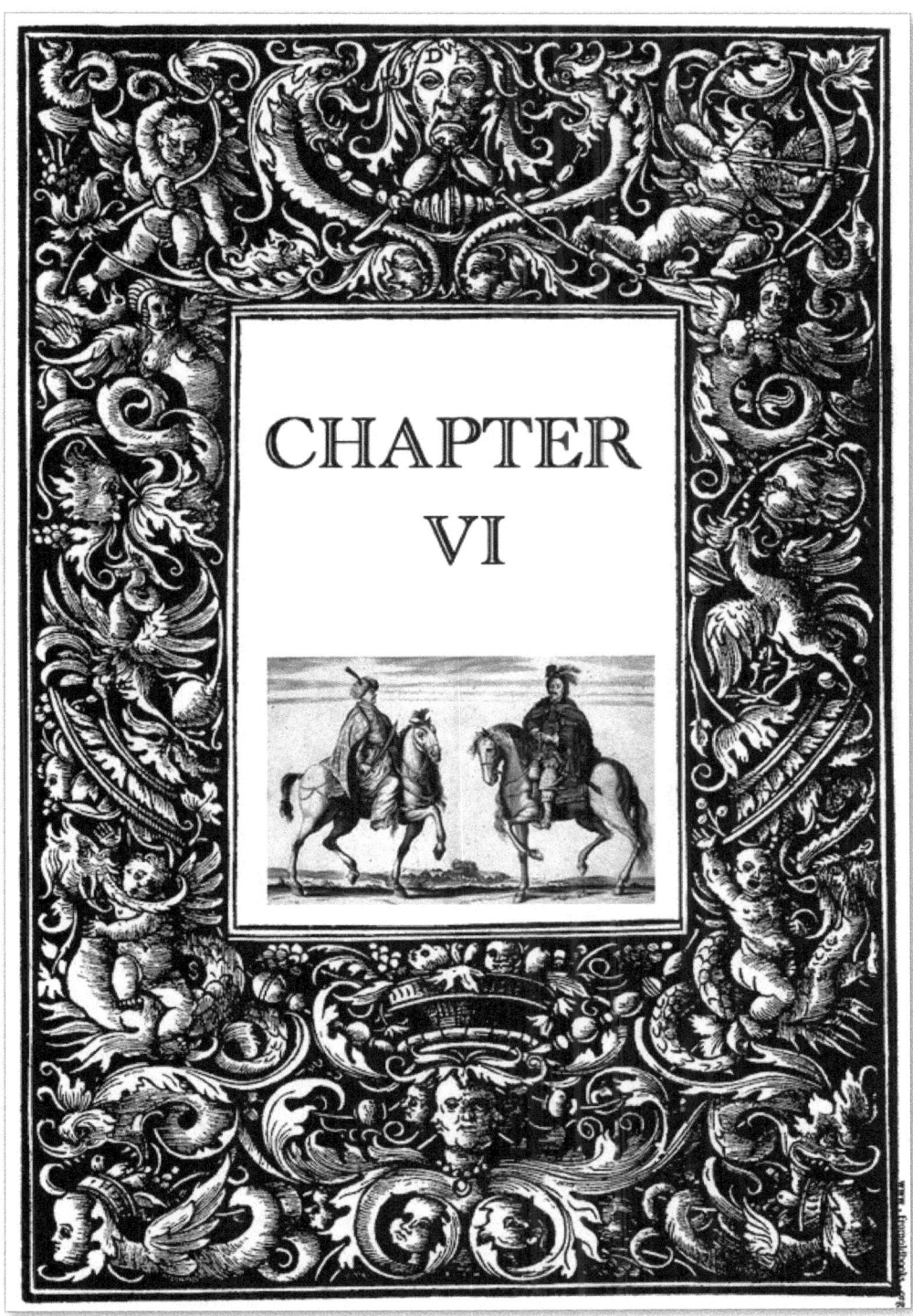

CHAPTER VI

▲ The Wiener Turkenbelagerung.

CHAPTER VI

There was no time to be lost indeed. The fortifications of Vienna were a mere heap of ruins. The Imperial Palace was battered to pieces. Nearly one whole quarter of the city was in ashes.

On the 3rd of September, the long contested Burg ravelin was yielded to the Turks.

On the 4th, the salient angle of the Burg bastion was blown into the air, and an attack was with difficulty repelled. On the 6th, a similar mine and assault following cumbered the Lowel bastion with ruin and with corpses. For a moment, the horse tails were planted upon the ramparts.

Driven back thence with difficulty, the Turks still clung to the Burg ravelin, and four pieces of cannon planted there, at frightfully close quarters, completed the ruin of the works. But no new attack came.

Informed of the advance of Lorraine, though still incredulous of the presence of Sobieski, the Vizier began to draw his troops towards the foot of the Kahlenberg. He still clung to the batteries and trenches; still kept the pick of his Janissaries grappling with the prize which but for him they might have already won.

He rejected the advice of the Pasha of Pesth, to withdraw across the Wien and fortify a camp on the Wienersberg, secure that if the Christians attacked and failed Vienna would fall.

He withdrew his troops indeed from the Leopoldstadt, and threw up some slight works towards the Kahlenberg, but remained other' wise irresolute, halting between his expected booty and her deliverer.

Sobieski had already taken the measure of his opponent. In reply to desponding views of Lorraine at Tuln, he had said, *"Be of good cheer which of us at the head of two hundred thousand men would have allowed this bridge to have been thrown within five leagues of his camp?"* To his wife he wrote, *"A commander who has thought neither of entrenching his camp, nor of concentrating his forces, but who lies encamped there as if we were one hundred miles off, is predestined to be beaten."*

Viewing the Turkish force from the Kahlenberg, he said to his soldiers, *"This man is badly encamped, he knows nothing of war; we shall beat him."*

It was , well for the Christians and for Vienna that none of the great warriors who had served the Porte was now in command. No man like Kiuprili, or even like Ibrahim *"the Devil"* the last Turkish commander against whom Sobieski had contended, was there, to use the fidelity of the Janissaries and the valour of the Spahis to advantage.

The march up the defiles of the Kahlenberg presented, even without interruptions, extraordinary difficulties. The king himself pushed forward to superintend the exploration of the way. He was so long parted from his Polish troops that they became anxious for his safety. He rejoined them at mid-day on the 11th, and encouraged them as they marched, or, as he says, rather climbed to the summit.

Some Saxon troops, first arriving with three guns, opened fire upon a Turkish detachment marching too late to secure the important position. The Turks retired, and the distant sound of the firing announced to Vienna the first tidings of deliverance.

It was not till the evening of the 11th, however, that the main body of the army had reached the ridge. Even then many had lagged behind; the paths were nearly impracticable for artillery, and the Germans abandoned many of their guns in despair between Tuln and the Kahlenberg.

But few pieces indeed were fired after the first beginning of the battle on the following day, Polish guns, for the most part, brought up by the vigour of the Grand Marshal of the Artillery, Kouski, the same officer who had directed the Polish field-pieces against the Turkish camp at Choczim. *"An hour before sunset"* September 11, as Sobieski and the generals stood at length upon the crest of the hill"they saw outspread before them one of the most magnificent yet terrible displays of human power which man has seen.

There lay the valley and the islands of the Danube, covered with an encampment, the sumptuousness of which seemed better suited for an excursion of pleasure than for the hardships of war. Within it stood an innumerable multitude of animals-horses, camels, and oxen. Two hundred thousand fighting men moved in order here and there, while along the foot of the hills below swarms of Tartars roamed at will.

A frightful cannonade was raging vigorously from the one side, in feeble reply from the other.

Beneath the canopy of smoke lay a great city, visible only by her spires and her pinnacles, which pierced the overwhelming cloud and flame.[8]

Sobieski estimated the force before him at one hundred thousand tents and three hundred thousand men. Including the non combatants, he was, perhaps, not far wrong; but the fighting men in the Turkish army by this time would be by many fewer than that number. One hundred and sixty-eight thousand men is the most which may be allowed from the muster-rolls found in the Vizier's tent, and that certainly exceeds the truth. t All around, except where in the encampment the magnificence of the invader was proudly flaunted in the face of the ruin that he had made, the prospect was desolated by war.

Whatever might be the fortune of the coming day, a generation at least must elapse before those suburbs are rebuilt, those villages restored and repeopled, those fields fully cultivated again.

The army felt that it lay with them, under God, to provide against that further extension of the ravage which would follow, should the bulwark of the Oesterreich, the Eastern March of the Empire, be forced by Hun and Tartar. Not distinguishable from the distance at which they stood, thousands of Christian captives lay in the encampment below. The morrow might deliver up the people of Vienna to a like fate with theirs. The city, as the king declared on entering it after the relief, could not have held out five days. As the wind now lifted the cloud of smoke, where should have been the fortifications, the eye could discern nothing but a circle of shapeless ruin, reaching from the Scottish gate to what had been the Burg bastion. Up to and on to it climbed the curving lines of the Turkish approaches. Sobieski had only hoped gradually to fight his way into a position whence he could communicate with the besieged, and he had arranged his plan of battle at Tuln with that idea. But the inequalities of the country between the Kahlenberg and Vienna, broken with vines, villages, small hills and hollow ways, together with the unexpectedly rapid development of the attack when once it began, seem to have interfered with his original disposition. His army occupied a front of half a Polish mile, or about an English mile and three quarters. It was drawn up in three supporting lines that faced south -eastward.

The first line of the right wing was composed of nineteen Polish (cavalry) divisions and four battalions; the second, of six Polish and eight Austrian divisions, and four Polish battalions; the third, of nine Polish, six Austrian, three German divisions, three Polish and one German battalion. The centre was composed in the first line of nine Austrian and eleven German divisions, and thirteen German battalions; in the second, of six German divisions, ten German and six Austrian battalions; in the third, of five German and two Austrian battalions. The left wing shewed in the first line, ten Austrian and five German divisions, and six Austrian battalions; in the second line, four German and eight Austrian divisions; in the third line, three German and seven Austrian battalions. Lubomirski with his irregular Poles was on the left; the Polish Field-Marshal, Jablonowski, commanded on the right; the Prince of Waldeck, with the Electors of Bavaria and Saxony, the centre; the Duke of Lorraine and Louis of Baden, with Counts Leslie and Caprara, were on the left.

The king was upon the right or right centre throughout the day. The total force, including detachments not actually engaged, was 46,700 cavalry and dragoons, 38,700 infantry; in all 85,400 men, with some irregulars, and 168 guns, many of them not in action at all. The dragoons fought on foot in the battle.[9]

The army was, roughly, one-third Poles, one-third Austrians, one-third Bavarians, Saxons, and other Germans. The fatigues of the march from Tuln would naturally diminish the number of effective soldiers on the day of battle; and the troops were not all in position when the evening of Saturday, September 11, fell. As the night however wore away, the rear guard gained the summit of the hills, and snatched a brief repose before the labours of the morrow. But for the king there was no rest.

The man whom the French ambassador had described as unable to ride, who was tormented certainly by wearing pains, after three days of incessant toil, passed a sleepless night preparatory to fourteen hours in the saddle upon the battle-field. The season of repose was dedicated to the duties of a general and the affection of a husband. At three a.m. on Sunday, the 12th, the king is again writing to his *bien-aimée Mariette*. He has

---

8 - The roll includes the forces of Tekeli, who was not in the Turkish camp at all, and takes no count of the last losses which the Turkish detachments had suffered, nor of the loss from desertion the night before the battle, when many of the irregulars went off with their booty.

The Turks had lost, according to this roll, 48,500 men before the battle .. -See Thurheim's "Starhemberg" pp. 150 and s.

9 - The dragoons were mounted infantry, using horses to reach the scene of action only. They carried the infantry weapons, sword and musket, but not pikes. The bayonet was just coming into use, but was still fixed in the muzzle of the gun, and had to be removed before firing.

been toiling all day in bringing his troops up the ravines.

"We are so thin" he writes *"We might run down the stags on the mountains."* As to the pomp or even comfort of a king, that is not to be thought of. *"All my luggage which we have got up here is in the two lightest carts."* He has some more upon mules, but has not seen them for forty-eight hours.

He had no thought of sleep; indeed, the thunder of the Turkish cannon made it impossible; and a gale of wind, which he describes as *"sufficient to blow the men off their horses"* bore the noise of their discharge with redoubled clamour to the relieving army. Moreover, the king writes, he must be in the saddle before daybreak, riding down from the right to the extreme left, to consult with Lorraine, opposite whom the enemy lies in force; not entrenched, he hopes, as on that side he means to break through to the city.

A two days' affair, at least, he thinks. Then, *"my eighth letter to your sixth"* he adds, with other familiar and gentle conversation, with tidings of her son and of other friends, but with no word of fear or of apprehension. He had made his will before setting out from Warsaw, but he entertained no thought of failure.

Then closing his wife's letter, the affectionate husband becomes again the heroic king and careful general. He rides from right to left along the lines, in that boisterous autumnal morning, makes the last dispositions with Lorraine, with him and with a few others takes again the Holy Communion from the hands of Marco d'Aviano before the sun has risen, and then returns to his post upon the right wing, ready for the advance that was to save Vienna. His next letter to his wife was dated *"September 13, night. The tents of the Vizier."*

▲ A Polish winged hussar

▲ Archers of the Guard of the Sultan (Solak Ortasi) with a pointed ak börk adorned with plumes. Their dolama is embellished with braid. Lead to the belt, in addition to the scimitar, the quiver with arrows and the kirban placed with the composite bow.
(2) Janissaries Aga (Yeniçeri Agasi) with flowing ceremonial robes. Wearing the old turban tulpend örf pumpkin-shaped, soon to be abandoned in favor of selimi turban.

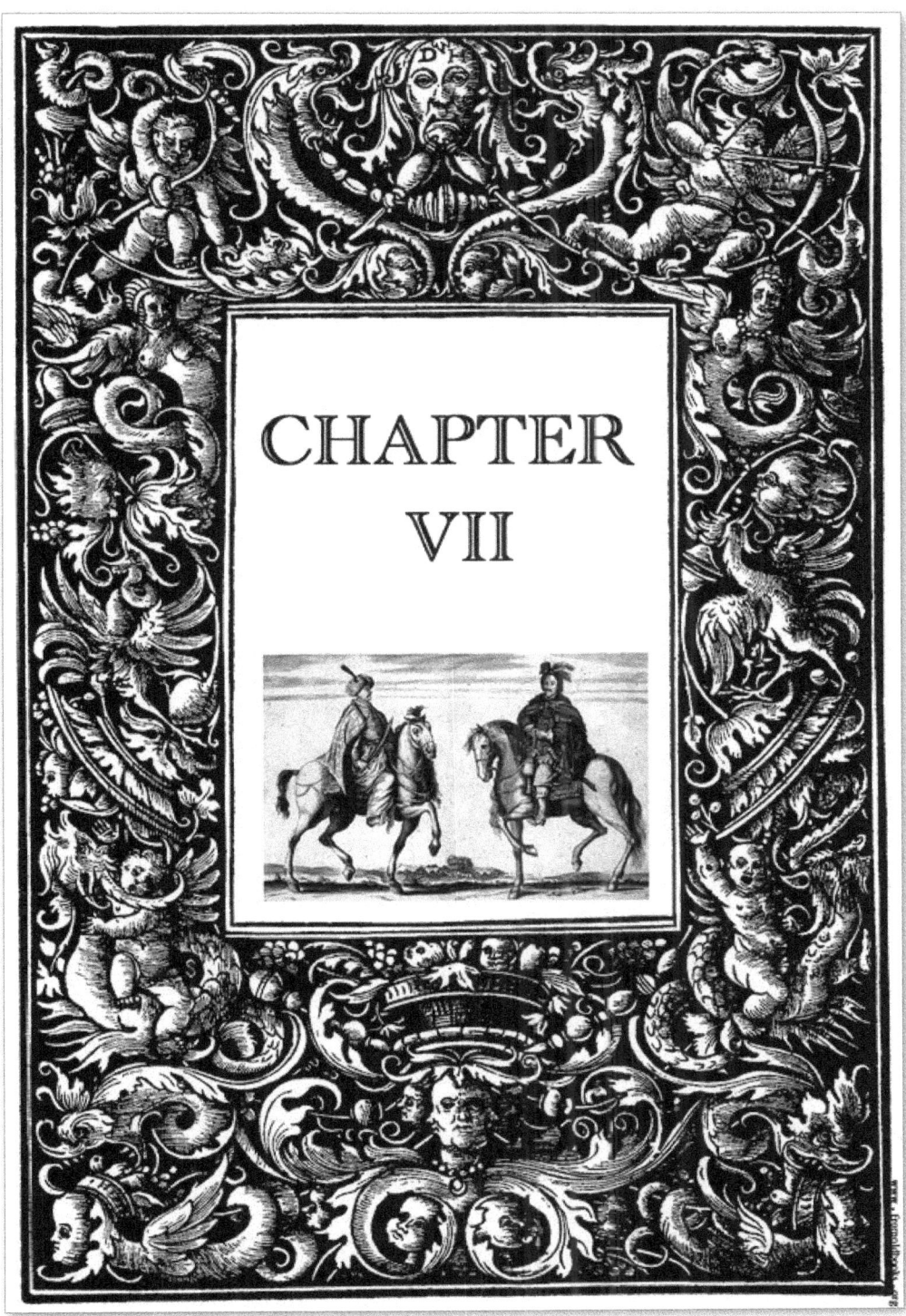

CHAPTER VII

▲ An Italian map of the siege of Vienna of 1683.

CHAPTER VII

The position of the Christian army on the Kahlenberg was, from the left wing, the nearest point, about foul' miles from Vienna. The centre and right were further removed. The intervening country, far from being a plain, as Sobieski had been led to believe when he formed his first plan of battle, is broken up into hillocks and little valleys, intersected by streams, full of vineyards, and interspersed with the ruins of numerous villages burnt by the Turks.

Beyond these lay the Turkish encampment and approaches, mingled with the vestiges of the suburbs destroyed by Starhemberg at the beginning of the siege.

The Turkish army was stretched over a front of about four miles from point to point, but slightly curving with the convex side towards the attacking force. Their right l'ested upon the Danube, and held the Nussberg before the villages of Nussdorf and Heiligenstaclt; their left reached towards Breitensee near the Wien, and the Tartars swarmed still further on the broken ground beyond. Their camp straggled in an irregular half-moon from the river above Vienna to beyond the Wien, and their troops were, at the beginning of the action, drawn up before it. Some hasty entrenchments had been thrown up by them here and there, of which the most considerable as a battery between Wahring, Gerstorf and Weinhaus; but the bulk of their artillery remained in their lines, pointed against the city, and the clamour of the ensuing battle was swelled by the continuous roar of their bombardment, kept up as on previous days.

In the trenches lay a great body of Janissaries; and the Turkish army was further weakened by the dispersal of Tartars and irregulars on the night before the fight, doubtful of the event, and anxious at any rate to secure their plunder. As the king had said, the Turks were badly posted, their camp was long and straggling, too valuable to be abandoned and not easy to defend. In case of a reverse, their right wing would run the risk of being driven into the Danube, or else have to fall back upon their centre and left, to the confusion of the whole army. Fighting with a river and a fortified city upon their flank and rear, repulse for them would mean certain disaster. But the incapacity of the Vizier could not be fully fathomed till the attack began.

We have the assurance of Sobieski himself that he hoped upon the first day merely to bring his army within striking distance of the enemy, and to establish his left well forward near the bank of the Danube, ready to deal a decisive blow, or to throw succour into Vienna on the morrow or following day.

He closed his letter to his wife in the grey of the windy morning of the 12th of September, ignorant that the decisive moment, bringing a victory greater than that of Choczim, was at hand. The Turks had pushed their outposts forward up the banks of the river, and soon after daybreak Lorraine upon the left was engaged, and the fight thickened as his attack towards Nussdorf and Heiligenstadt was developed.

Eugene of Savoy began his distinguished career in arms by carrying tidings from Lorraine to the king that the battle had commenced in earnest. Eugene, barely twenty, had left Paris that year, slighted by Louis, and had entered the service of the Emperor. His memoirs dismiss briefly this his first essay in war.

The confusion of that day can be but confusedly described. The Poles, who had clambered up to the Leopoldsberg - I know not why-went down again like madmen and fought like lions. The Turks, encamped where I threw up lines in 1703, did not know which way to front, neglected the eminences, and behaved like idiots.[10]

The young aide de-camp, carrying orders through the hottest of the fire, could not yet penetrate the system which underlay the apparent confusion of the march and battle. Advancing in columns with a comparatively narrow front down the difficult slope of the hills, the infantry gradually deployed right and left upon the lower ground, while the cavalry of the second line advanced to fill the gaps thus left in the foremost. The Turks resisted gallantly, but they were principally dismounted Spahis, not a match for Lorraine's favourite troops,

---

10 - In 1717 Eugene, in like case with the Vizier now, was besieging Belgrade, and was himself surrounded by a large Turkish army. However, he defeated the relieving army and took the city.

the German foot, though regaining their horses they would retreat with great rapidity, to again dismount, and again resist, as each favourable position offered itself. The fighting was obstinate, and the losses heavy upon both sides, but the tide of fight rolled steadily towards Vienna.

The Germans carried the height of the Nussberg, above Nussdorf, and their guns planted there disordered the whole of the Turkish right with their plunging fire. Osman Ogoli, Pasha of Kutaya, the Turkish general of division, pushed forward three columns in a counter-attack, boldly and skilfully directed.

The Imperial infantry were shaken, but five Saxon battalions, inclining to their left from the Christian centre, checked in turn the onset of the Ottomans, and restored the current of the battle.

But had the whole force of the enemy been commanded as their right wing, the allies would scarcely that night have been greeted in Vienna. No false move in the advance escaped the skill of Osman.

As the Turkish attack recoiled, the Prince of Croy had dashed forward with two battalions to carry with a rush the village of Nussdorf. Checked and overwhelmed, he fell back again, himself, wounded, his brother slain. Louis of Baden, with his dismounted dragoons, came up to the rescue, and checked the pursuing enemy. As they recoiled slowly the fight grew fiercer, and then more stationary about Nussdorf and about Dobling. Houses, gardens, and vineyards formed a series of entrenchments, sharply attacked and obstinately defended. A third time the fiery valour of the Turks, charging home with their sabres among the pikes and muskets, disordered the allies, and all but regained the summit of the Nussberg. Again the superior cohesion of the Christians prevailed, and the Turkish column outflanked fell back, still stubbornly contesting every foot of ground. From the long extended centre and left of their line no support came to them, as the Vizier in anxious irresolution expected the advance of the centre of the allies and of the Poles upon their right. His infatuation, moreover, had kept in the batteries the bulk of his artillery, and in the trenches the best of his Janissaries.

In dire want of the guns, which roared idly upon the already shattered defences of the city, Osman was driven through Nussdorf and through Heiligenstadt, upon the fortified defiles of Dobling, where at last a battery of ten guns and a force of Janissaries opposed a steadier resistance to the advancing Germans.

It was now noon. Lorraine had already won the position which had been marked out for his achievement for the day, and slackened his attack while he reformed his victorious battalions. The centre and right of the Christian army, separated by a longer distance from their foes, had been slowly gaining the field of action, and had scarce fired a shot nor struck a blow, except for the support accorded to the left by the centre.

The whole of the infantry and cavalry had at mid day gained the positions assigned to them, and, in the absence of most of his artillery, Sobieski would have hesitated to continue his advance had not his lines, upon the left especially, become so deeply involved that it was difficult to suspend the conflict for long. Yet a momentary lull succeeded to the sharp sounds of close combat. A sultry autumn day had followed the boisterous night and morning, and the heat was oppressive. [11]

The Poles upon the right halted and snatched a hasty meal from the provisions they had brought with them. But as the rattle of the small arms and the clash of weapons died away, the roar of the battering guns and the answering fire of the city rose in overwhelming distinctness. Behind the smoky veil, Starhemberg and his gallant garrison could perchance barely guess, by sounds of conflict, the progress of their deliverers.

Tidings from the watch-chair on St. Stephen's would spread alternate hope and despair among the citizens. The fate of Vienna trembled in the balance. The garrison stood ready in the breaches, the rest of the inhabitants cowered upon the housetops to watch, or knelt in the churches to pray; but to the Vizier came swiftly tidings of the foe with whom he had to deal, the foe whose presence he had obstinately refused to credit.

Reforming after their brief delay, the Polish cavalry in gorgeous arms came flashing from the woods and defiles near Dornbach on his left. Those who had before fought against him, knew the plume raised upon a spear point, the shield borne before him, the banderolles on the lances of his body guard, which declared the presence of the terrible Sobieski. *"By Allah, but the king is really among them"* cried Gieray, Khan of the Crimea. And all doubt was at an end as the shout of *"Virat Sobieski"* rolled along the Christian lines, in dread and significant answer to the discordant clamour of the Infidels.

---

11 - There is a proverb *"Vienna aut venenosa aut ventosa."* She was giving to her deliverers successive displays of her character.

▲ Gwardia Koronna. The reform introduced by Ladislaus IV Vasa changed the Guard of the Crown of Poland in a private army of Western model with Pikemen (1), Musketeers (2) and Cuirassiers (4).
The uniforms reproduced the yellow-and-blue of the Vasa of Sweden. Most of the levers of the Guard, during the reign of Ladislaus and his brother John Casimir, came from the Germanic lands of the Confederation (fond. Livonia and Courland). and were commanded by Mercenaries Officers (3) formed on the stage of the Thirty Years War.

Profiting, however, by the interruption in the battle, the Vizier had reformed his line, brought up infantry from the trenches, and now directed his attack upon the Poles and the most formidable of his opponents, hoping by their overthrow to change the fortune of the day, while the Imperialists and Saxons still halted before his entrenchments at Dobling. The Turks advanced with courage.

For a moment a regiment of Polish lancers were thrown into confusion, and the officers, members of the nobility of Poland, who strove to rally their lines, fell; but Waldeck, moving up his Bavarians from the centre, restored the fight. The attack was defeated, and advancing in turn the headlong valour of the Poles drove the Turks back from point to point, over the Alserbach and its branches upon the confines of their camp.

To relieve the pressure upon the right and centre, Lorraine had renewed his attack with the left of the allies. Horses and men had recovered breath and order, and their artillery had moved up in support.

The defiles of Dobling were cleared by the Saxons; and at about four or five o'clock the Turkish redoubt before Wahring was carried by Louis of Baden with his dismounted dragoons.

Falling back in confusion upon their approaches and batteries, the Turks desperately endeavoured, too late, to turn the siege guns upon the enemy, whose advance now threatened them upon all sides.

The caution of Sobieski had, up to the last moment, inclined him to respect the superior numbers and the desperation of his foes, and to rest content with the advantage won; but now, in the growing confusion, he saw that the decisive hour had arrived. The Elector of Bavaria and the Prince of Waldeck hastening from the centre already saluted him as conqueror. The desperate efforts of the Vizier to gain room by moving troops towards his left from the centre, and so extending his lines beyond the Polish right, served but to increase the confusion.

The Field Marshal Jablonowski covered that wing, and the Queen of Poland's brother, the Count de Maligni, pushing forward with infantry, seized a mound, whence his musketry fire dominated the spot where the Vizier stood. The last shots were fired from the two or three cannon which had kept pace with the advance.

A French officer rammed home the last charge with his gloves, his wig, and a packet of French papers.

Already the roads to Hungary were thronged with fugitives, whose course was marked by dust in columns, when the king decided to seize the victory all but in his grasp already. *"Non nobis, non nobis, Domine exercituum, sed Nomini Tuo des gloriarm"*, he cried in answer to the congratulations of his friends, as he began the decisive movement. Concentrating as rapidly as possible the bulk of the cavalry of the whole army, German and Polish, upon the right wing, he led them to the charge, directly upon the spot where the Vizier with blows, tears, and curses, was endeavouring to rally the soldiers, whom his own ill-conduct had deprived of their wonted valour.

The Turkish infantry without pikes, their cavalry without heavy armour, were incapable of withstanding the shock of the heavy German cuirassiers, or of arresting the rush of the Polish nobles, whose spears, as they boasted to their kings, would uphold the heavens should they fall.

Their king at their head, they came down like a whirlwind to the shout of *"God preserve Poland."* The spears of the first line were splintered against the few who awaited them, but their onset was irresistible. Spahis and Janissaries, Tartars and Christian allies alike went down before the Polish lances, or turned and fled in headlong confusion.

The old Pasha of Pesth, the greatest of the Turkish warriors in reputation, had fled already. The Pashas of Aleppo and of Silistria perished in the melée. *"Can you not help me ?"* cried the Vizier, turning to the Khan of the Crimea.

"No" was the reply; *"I know the King of Poland well, it is impossible to resist him; think only of flight."* [12]

Away through the wasted borders of Austria, away to the Hungarian frontier, to their army that lay before Raab, poured the fugitives. There seldom has been a deliverance more complete and more decisive.

The terror which had so long weighed upon Eastern Christendom was dissolved in that headlong rout. It was more than the scattering of an army; the strength of an empire was dissipated on that day.

---

12 - Sobieski's letter of September 13. He must have heard of the conversation from the Vizier's attendants taken in his encampment.

Resources which had been accumulating for years were destroyed; and such an expedition, so numerous and so well furnished, never was sent forth by the Ottoman again. The victory lacked nothing to render it more striking, either in suddenness, in completeness, or in situation. The whole action had been comprised in the hours between sunrise and sunset, before the gates of one of the greatest capitals in Europe.

We may borrow indeed the words of Eugene, used in his despatch describing the last victory of the war at Zenta, to picture the last hours of that evening before Vienna. For upon the summits of the Weiner-Wald, whence the allies had descended that morning to a yet doubtful field the sun seemed to linger, loath to leave the day, until his rays had illumined to the end the triumph of the glorious arms of Poland and of the Empire. There was no want of individual courage among the Turks. "They made the best retreat you can conceive" wrote the king, for hard pressed they would turn sword in hand upon their pursuers.

But the head which should have directed that courage was wanting; and for that want they were a gallant mob, but no longer an army. Grateful for the result though we may be, there is something pathetic in the magnificent valour of a race of soldiers being frustrated by such incapacity. The Christians exhausted by the toils of the last few days, could not pursue to any distance.

The Imperial General Dunewald indeed with a few squadrons of Austrians and Poles, the stoutest steeds or the keenest riders, despising both plunder and fatigue, pushed straight on through the twilight to Enzersdorf, where the road crossed the stream of the Fischa, ten miles from Vienna, and there bursting on the line of flight made a slaughter of the fugitives, which showed how much they owed to the night and to the weariness of their conquerors. But there was no general pursuit on the part of the allies.

Their commanders were doubtful of the full extent of their victory, and feared lest from such a multitude some part might rally and destroy the too eager followers whom they still outnumbered.

But without pursuit their work was done. At seven, Louis of Baden had opened a communication with the besieged, and the garrison sallying forth joined the relieving army in the slaughter of the Janissaries who had remained, neglected or forgotten, in the trenches. Even then one miner was found, doggedly toiling in his gallery beneath the ramparts, ignorant of the flight or death of his companions; perhaps from among so many the last staunch soldier of the Prophet.

I cannot conceive, wrote Sobieski, how they can carry on the war after such a loss of materiel. The whole of the artillery of the Turks, their munitions, and their baggage were the spoil of the victors.

Three hundred and ten pieces of cannon, twenty thousand animals, nine thousand carriages, one hundred and twenty-five thousand tents, five million pounds of powder are enumerated.

The holy standard of the Prophet had been saved, but the standard of the Vizier, mistaken for it, was sent to the Pope by the conqueror, while his gilded stirrups were despatched at once to Poland to the Queen, as a token of victory. Never, perhaps, since Alexander stood a victor at Issus in the tents of Darius, or the Greeks stormed the Persian camp at Platea, had an European army entered upon such spoil.

Much money had been saved by the Turks in their flight; but precious stuffs and jewelled arms, belts thick with diamonds, intended to encircle the fair captives of Vienna, the varied plunder of many a castle of Hungary and of Lower Austria, were found piled in the encampment.

In the Vizier's quarters were gardens laid out with baths and fountains, a menagerie, even a rabbit warren. His encampment alone formed a labyrinth of tents, by itself of the circumference of a little town, and with its contents declared the character of its late owner. An ostrich, previously taken from an Imperial castle, was found beheaded to prevent recapture. A parrot, more fortunate, escaped upon the wing.

The Polish envoy was discovered in the camp in chains, forgotten during the turmoil, and thus saved from the death promised him if his master should take the field. The Imperial agent at the Porte, Kunitz, had escaped into the town during the battle; but the mass of Christian captives had not been so happy.

Before the battle the Vizier had ordered a general massacre of prisoners, and the camp was cumbered with the bodies of men, women, and children, but for the most part of women, foully slaughtered.

The benevolent energy of the Bishop of Neustadt, above-mentioned, found employment in caring for five hundred children, who had, with their mothers in a few cases, escaped the sword.

The night was passed in the camp by the victors, who were intent on securing their victory or their plunder. Not till the following morning did the king meet Lorraine and exchange congratulations upon their success.

Then, with the Commandant Starhemberg, they entered the city, passing over those well-contested breaches, which but for them might have been that day trodden by the Janissaries.

They repaired to the churches for a solemn thanksgiving. Sobieski himself sang the *Te Deum* in one of them. Nothing could exceed the enthusiastic gratitude of the people, who barely allowed a passage to the horse of their deliverer. The priest, after the *Te Deum* ended, by a happy inspiration or plagiarism, gave out the words *"There was a man sent from God, whose name was John."*[13] A salute of three hundred guns proclaimed the victory far and wide, and the shouts of *"Vivat Sobieski!"*

that filled the city out-thundered the thunder of the cannon. Their walls were a chaos, their habitations a ruin, but the citizens rejoiced as those rejoice whom the Lord hath redeemed and delivered from the hand of the enemy.

They were as men released not only from the sword, pestilence, and famine, but from prison besides.

They poured forth to taste again the sweets of liberty, wondered at the trenches, or joined in the pillage of the camp, where the air was already sickening from the thousands of the slain, and foul from the refuse of the barbaric encampment. But amid all the popular rejoicing, the king could not but observe the coldness of the magistracy.

The Emperor could not endure that any but himself should triumph in Vienna, and his feelings were reflected in his servants. On hearing of the victory he had returned to the neighbourhood of the city.

A council was held to settle the weighty point as to how the elective Emperor was to receive the elective King.

"With open arms, since he has saved the Empire" said Lorraine; but Leopold would not descend to such an indecorum.

He strove to avoid a meeting with the deliverer of his capital, and when the meeting was arranged could barely speak a few cold words in Latin, well answered by Sobieski, who, saying *"I am happy, Sire, to have been able to render you this slight service"* turned his horse, saluted, and rode away.

A few complimentary presents to Prince James and to the Polish nobles did not efface the impression of ingratitude.

The German writers minimize the coldness of the Emperor, but Sobieski was at the moment undoubtedly aggrieved, and others were discontented.

---

13 - It was the exclamation of the Pope, Pius V, on hearing of the victory of Don John of Austria over the Turks at Lepanto, in 1571.

▲ Polish pikemen (late XVII century) Already under the walls of Vienna in 1683, the Polish pikemen were the most obvious result of the now heavy western contamination in Commonwealth's costume of war.
The soldiers depicted wearing typical Polish clothes with fur edging and are armed with pistol, saber and ax supporting the pike.

▲ Turkish jannissaries with blow and lance.

CHAPTER VIII

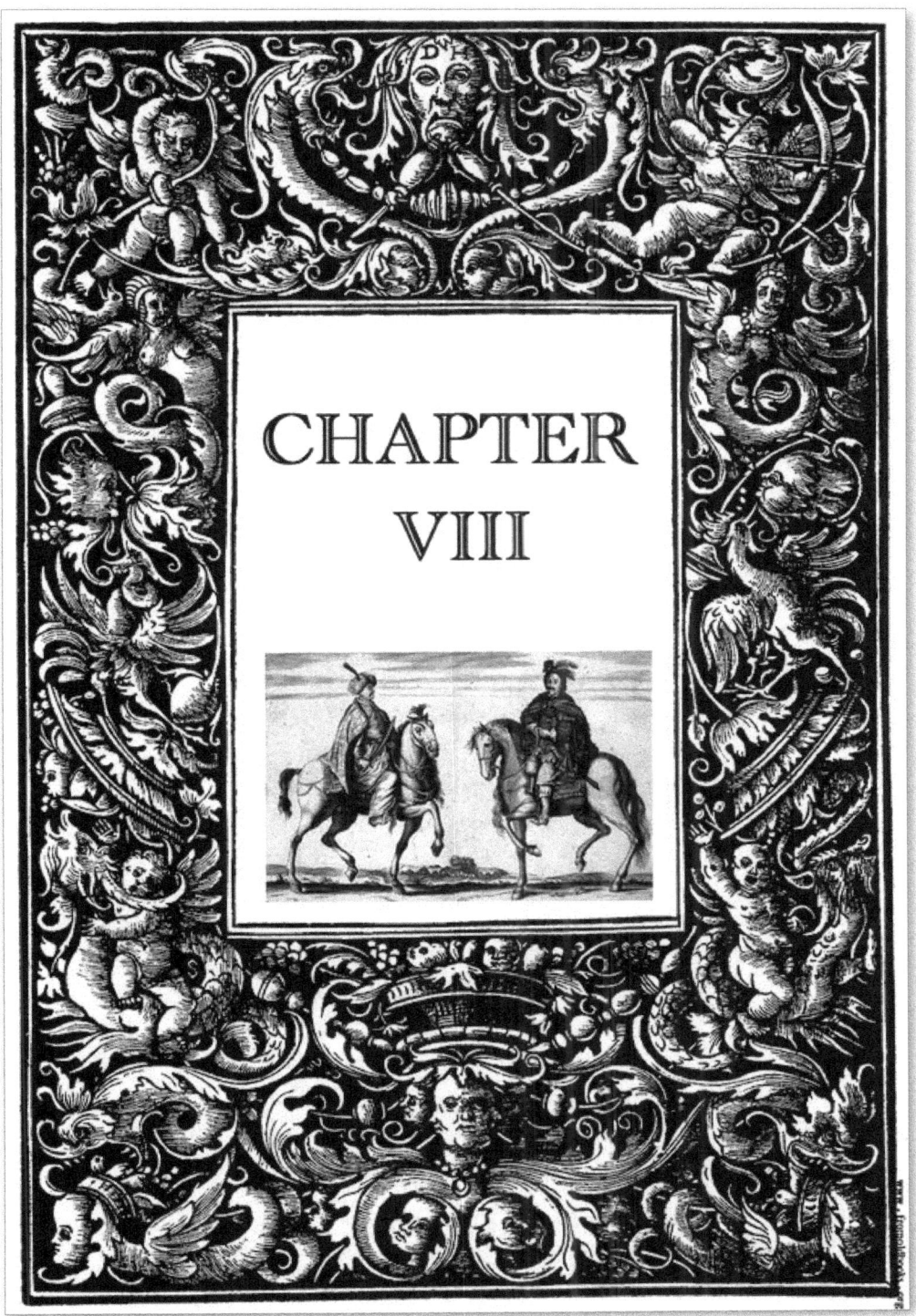

▲ Turkish cavalryman in the battle of Vienna.

CHAPTER VIII

Neglected and distrusted by the sovereign whom he had delivered, Sobieski found consolation in detailing his victory, his spoil, and his wrongs alike to his wife. We find the great soldier again, in the full flush of his victory, writing indefatigably to his Mariette.

It is on the night of the 13th, in the Vizier's late quarters, in the camp still cumbered with the slaughter of the combatants and of prisoners. The loss had been heavy in the fighting upon both sides, he tells us; and such an estimate, formed at such a moment by the victorious general, by far outweighs the accounts by which the French above all tried to minimize the slaughter made, and with it the greatness of the victory won. 14

He begins his letter: *"God be blessed for ever. He has given victory to our people; He has given them such a triumph that past ages have not seen the like."*

All around, the explosions of the Turkish ammunition, fired by the plunderers from city and army, "make a din like the last judgment." He plunges into a description of the riches that the camp contains. *"The Vizier has made me his heir; he has done everything en galant homme."* *"You cannot say to me, "You are no warrior,"* as the Tartar women say to their husbands when they return empty-handed. *"For two nights and a day plunder has gone on at will; even the townsfolk have taken their share, and I am sure that there is enough left for eight days more. The plunder we got at Choczim was nothing to this."* There was a touch of the barbaric chieftain in the Polish king, and he keenly enjoyed not merely the victory, but the spoil which he had won.

At the end of the seventeenth century, the character of this general of the school of Montecuccoli, this admired of Condé, recalls to us at once the ardour of a crusader, and the affectionate rapacity of a moss-trooper, reserving the richest plunder of a foray to deck his wife at home. He exults in the belts and in the watches studded with jewels, the stuffs and the embroideries, which are to adorn his wife's boudoir.

But he is still bent on action. *"We must march to-morrow for Hungary"* he says, *"and start at the double, to escape the smell of the camp and its refuse, with the thousands of bodies of men and of animals lying unburied."* One letter, at least, he had despatched before writing to his wife.

He knew well the feelings with which the King of France would regard the salvation of the Empire, and the setting free of the attention of Germany to be directed to his own designs.

In Sobieski's own words to his wife, he thus reveals his triumph over the French king, whose intrigues had been ceaselessly directed to prevent his coming: *"I have written to the King of France; I have told him that it was to him especially, as to the Most Christian King, that I felt bound to convey the information of the battle that we have won, and of the safety of Christendom."* This letter remained unanswered.

It is said that the proofs of Louis' dealings with the Turks had at that moment passed into the hands of the victors, amid the plunder of the Vizier's quarters. No sooner had Louis heard that the intrigues of his agents had failed, and that Sobieski was actually in the field, than his armies were let loose upon the Spanish Netherlands. Unable to anticipate the victory at Vienna, the French revenged it by seizing Courtrai and Dixmunde in the autumn, and bombarding Luxemburg before the end of the year.

The French nobility had been forbidden to hasten to the defence of Christendom; and now were inclined to depreciate, at least in words, the victory they had not shared. Amidst the general chorus of admiration and of

---

14 - A moderate estimate of the Christian loss is five thousand men, or about one fifteenth of those on the field; a loss in about the same proportion as that of both sides at Sadowa. The Poles alone confessed to the loss of one hundred officers killed, and they were neither so long nor so hotly engaged as the left wing. The loss of the centre was probably less. Thurheim and Schimmer give of the allies four thousand, and twenty five thousand Turks; but the latter figures are quite uncertain, and the Christians made the least of their losses. As the fight was so much hand to hand, with little artillery fire, it would resemble ancient battles, where the loss of the vanquished was always disproportionately large. The memoirs of the Duke of Lorraine simply say, that "for about three hours the fighting was very bloody upon both sides." Fighting, however, had begun soon after daybreak, and the pursuit lasted till nightfall.

thankfulness, which rose from Europe, in France, and in France alone, were the deeds of Sobieski slighted. He had cut in pieces not only the Turks, but the prophecies which had filled Paris of the approaching downfall of the house of Austria. The allies of that house took a bolder tone; Spain talked of the declaration of that war against Louis which he had provoked for so long; the United Provinces listened to the warlike councils of the Prince of Orange; the Emperor spoke decidedly of succouring all his friends. Far different was to be the progress of Louis aggressions upon Germany, now that the overmastering fear of Turkish invasion was done away with, and the Turkish hold upon Hungary loosened.

The alliance of Laxenberg and the other leagues were now to ripen into the great confederacy of Augsburg and the Grand Alliance. Upon the Ottoman power the effect of the victory was decisive.

Turkish rule in Hungary had received a blow from which it never recovered. It is true that Sobieski, advancing rashly with his cavalry alone, shortly involved himself in a disaster, near the bridge of the Danube, opposite Gran.

The king himself had to ride for his life from the Turkish horsemen. The check, however, was avenged by the complete destruction of the force which had inflicted it; and the fortress of Gran, the most important place upon that side of Hungary, became the prize of the conqueror. The views of Sobieski embraced the reduction of Buda, and, perhaps, of the whole of Hungary, in this campaign. But this was forbidden by the lateness of the season, still more by the jealousy of the Emperor.

The king warred against the Turks, but not against the Hungarians. He sympathized with their efforts to regain their liberties, and strove to reconcile rather than to subdue Tekeli. Leopold was fearful of the establishment of a Polish interest in the country, and showed a studied neglect of his allies. But had other causes allowed, the insubordination of the Poles would have prevented further conquests.

The Polish nobility, the political masters of their king, were foremost in clamouring for a return to their native country. A prolonged career of conquest was impossible at the head of such a State and army.

The hopes of a Hungarian alliance died away. Tekeli, after much hesitation, refused to enter into the negotiations which the king proposed; and reluctantly the deliverer of Christendom withdrew through Upper Hungary into Poland again, reducing some towns upon the road, but leaving his great work half done.

His army melted in his hands. The tardy Lithuanians, too late for the fighting, arrived to add to his vexation in Mora via, where they disgraced their country by pillaging the people whom they had not helped to save.

But Sobieski was not alone in suffering from the Emperor's ingratitude. Starhemberg, the defender of the city, was deservedly rewarded; but most of the others, from Lorraine downwards, who had participated in the battle, had little recompense for their services. Even the ardour of the Elector of Bavaria was for a time cooled by the coolness of the Emperor, though he returned again to the service of his future father-in-law. The Elector of Saxony, Waldeck, and others left the scene of the campaign to enjoy their triumph, or to plunge into other enterprises; but under Lorraine, and a series of generals, culminating in that Eugene of Savoy, who had seen his first service at Vienna, the Turks were driven foot by foot from Hungary. Kara Mustapha shortly paid for his defeat, as Ottoman commanders did pay with his head, suffering not unjustly. But his successors, though less incompetent, were scarcely on the whole more fortunate than he. In vain a new Kiuprili was found to head the Turkish armies and to reform the Turkish State.

A short gleam of success under his leadership was ended by his death in battle. In vain a Sultan, Mustapha II, again appeared himself at the head of his armies. The means of warfare of the Ottomans were to a great extent expended and lost beyond repair in the great disaster at Vienna. New enemies rose up against them in their weakness. Russia in the Ukraine, Venice in the Morea and in Dalmatia, began conquests at the expense of the Porte. The war indeed dragged on, delayed by the renewed contest between France and the Augsburg league; but the very weakness of Austria served merely to show more clearly the fallen fortunes of the Turks, who could make no lasting stand against her. Steadily upon the whole the fortunes of the Ottomans declined, though it was not till the great victory of Eugene at Zenta, in 1697, that they 'were driven reluctantly to treat. The peace signed at Carlowitz, in 1699, illustrates the altered relations of Europe since the beginning of the war, when the Turks had been a menace to Germany. For the first time, an European conference considered the affairs of Turkey.

England and Holland were mediators of the peace, that the Emperor might be more free to act with them in the coming war of the Spanish Succession. Sobieski had nearly three years earlier become a memory, with his victories, his schemes, and his disappointments, in the grave; and with him ended the ever unstable greatness of Poland. Another yet more notable northern sovereign, Peter the Czar, was a party to the negotiations.

Everywhere was territory rent from Turkey. To Austria, she yielded nearly all of Hungary and Transylvania, with most of the Sclavonian lands between the Save and the Drave; to Poland, she gave up Podolia; to Russia, Azof; to Venice, the Morea and parts of Dalmatia. One point she proudly refused to yield.

The Hungarian Tekeli and his friends, who had sought her hospitality, were retained by her, safe from the vengeance of the Emperor; as in 1849 other Hungarian exiles were shielded by the Turks, against the vengeance of Austria and of Russia combined. This was the first peace which had permanently reduced the frontiers of the Ottomans; it marked the termination of the last of the great Mohammedan aggressions upon Christendom; it saw the end of the secret understandings by which, since the days of Francis 1.

France had endeavoured to use Turkey for the subversion of Austria and for the ends of her own ambition. The complete reversal of the former positions of the combatants, the disastrous termination of the war for Turkey, the rolling away of the stone of Tantalus that hung above their heads, the intolerable woe for the Germans, the far-reaching results of the struggle in the future history of Europe-all are traceable to the day when the genius of Sobieski marked triumphantly, from the windy heights of the Kahlenberg, that fatal incapacity which should open for him the way, as victorious deliverer, to the foot of the ruined ramparts of Vienna. But naturally, before concluding our consideration of the subject, we ask what gain did Poland, or the King of Poland, gather from the enterprise in which he had played so glorious a part? For a few months he was the centre of the admiring eyes of Christendom. *"L'empire du monde vous serait dù si le ciel l'eut reserve à un seul potentat"*, wrote Christina of Sweden from Rome, not without a glance at the pretensions of Louis XIV to supremacy, and of Leopold to an imperial primacy in Europe.

Never before had Poland filled so great a place in the eyes of the world. The cautious Venetians sought her special alliance. In the language of diplomacy she was Republica Serenissima; but untroubled she never was, and her greatness was of short duration. It is true that the frontiers of the State were relieved of a constant fear. The Turks were for the time broken, the Tartars were crushed, the Cossacks of the Ukraine again reduced to submission. But Sobieski had fought and had conquered for others. His country was incapable of gathering the fruits of victory; incapable of prolonged effort, and therefore of lasting success. At the peace of Carlowitz, Podolia, with the fortress of Kaminiec, was recovered; but Moldavia had been in vain invaded by the Poles; and the Turks, it was soon seen, were beaten for the benefit of Austria; the Tartars for the benefit of Russia.

The King of Poland, alive to the shortcomings of his countrymen, was unable to correct them. A man who was at least the most eminent soldier, general we may not say, of Europe; a man who above all others living fulfilled the character of a hero; a king who had saved his country; a husband who was devoted to his wife, found himself thwarted by his subjects, and distracted by quarrels in his family.

No doubt he laboured to render the crown hereditary in his house, a service to his country it would have been had he succeeded; but the jealousy of the Poles, still more that of the neighbouring sovereigns, and to some extent the misconduct of his wife, rendered this impossible. He found himself the object of an empty respect, but the wielder of no authority; he saw his country without order, without steadiness of purpose, unable to follow any settled policy in conjunction either with France or with the enemies of France.

The factions of the Diet left him without soldiers and without money. Not for the first, but nearly for the last time, the Poles were victorious in battle, but were destined to fail woefully in attaining the objects of war. The end was not far off. Sobieski was followed by a foreigner upon the throne, and within ten years of his death, Charles XII of Sweden was disposing as a conqueror of the crown of Poland. The prey to the ambition of her neighbours his country has remained, now like her king a memory, to serve as a lesson of the consequences of the disregard of those restraints and of that self-control which alone can render freedom safe and liberty a blessing.

For want of these her place has vanished from the map of Europe, sooner even than that of the foe whom she destroyed.

THE END

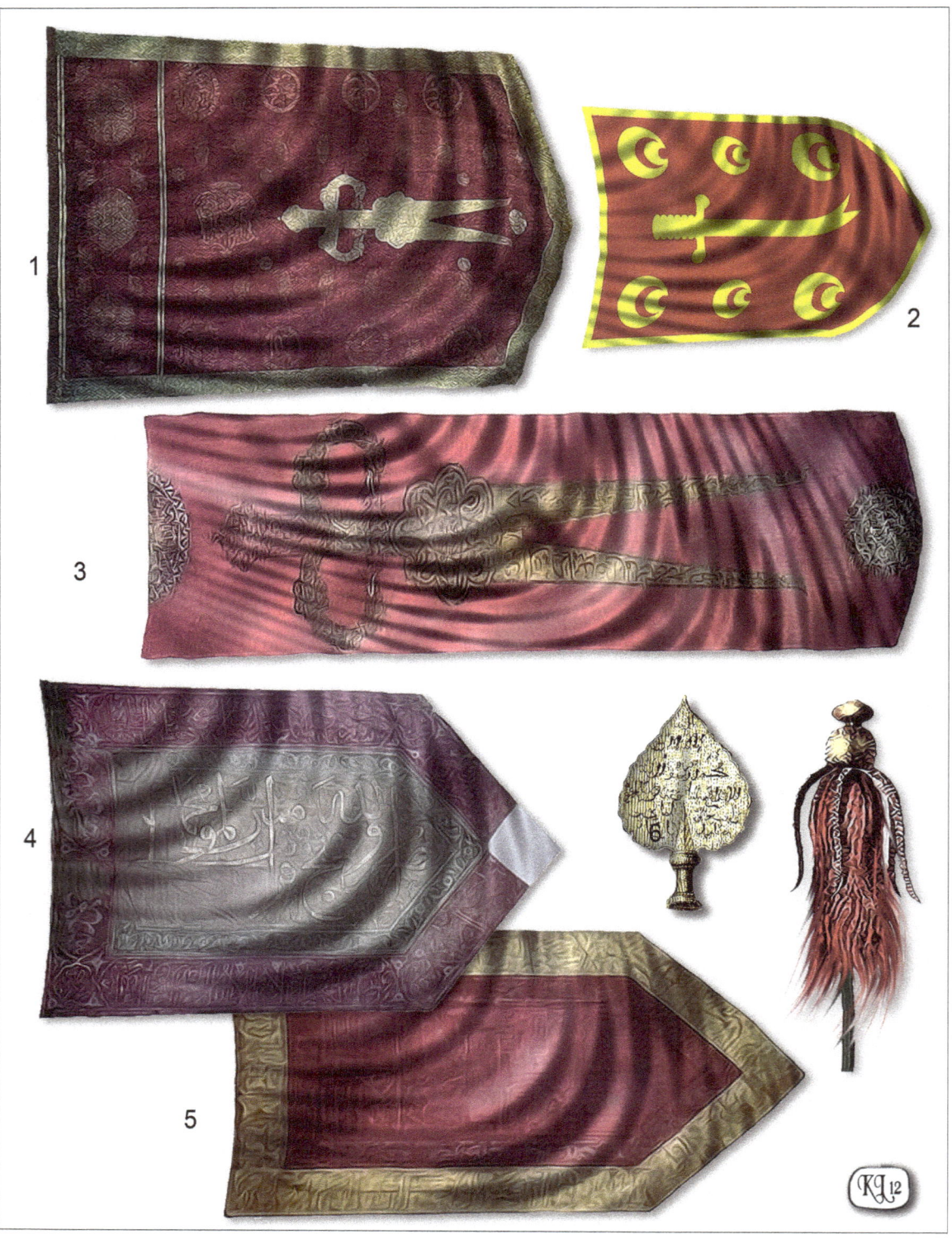

▲ Ottoman flags and banners 1-5 Banners of war (Sanchak) of the Ottoman Empire 3 is a reconstruction, distinguished by the color crimson, the Koranic inscriptions in Arabic and the symbol of the sacred double-headed sword Zulfiqar, the legendary weapon of the Prophet and symbol of 'militant Islam as much as the Kapukulu. 6 Tug with horsehair dyed red and a standard brass-shaped spire

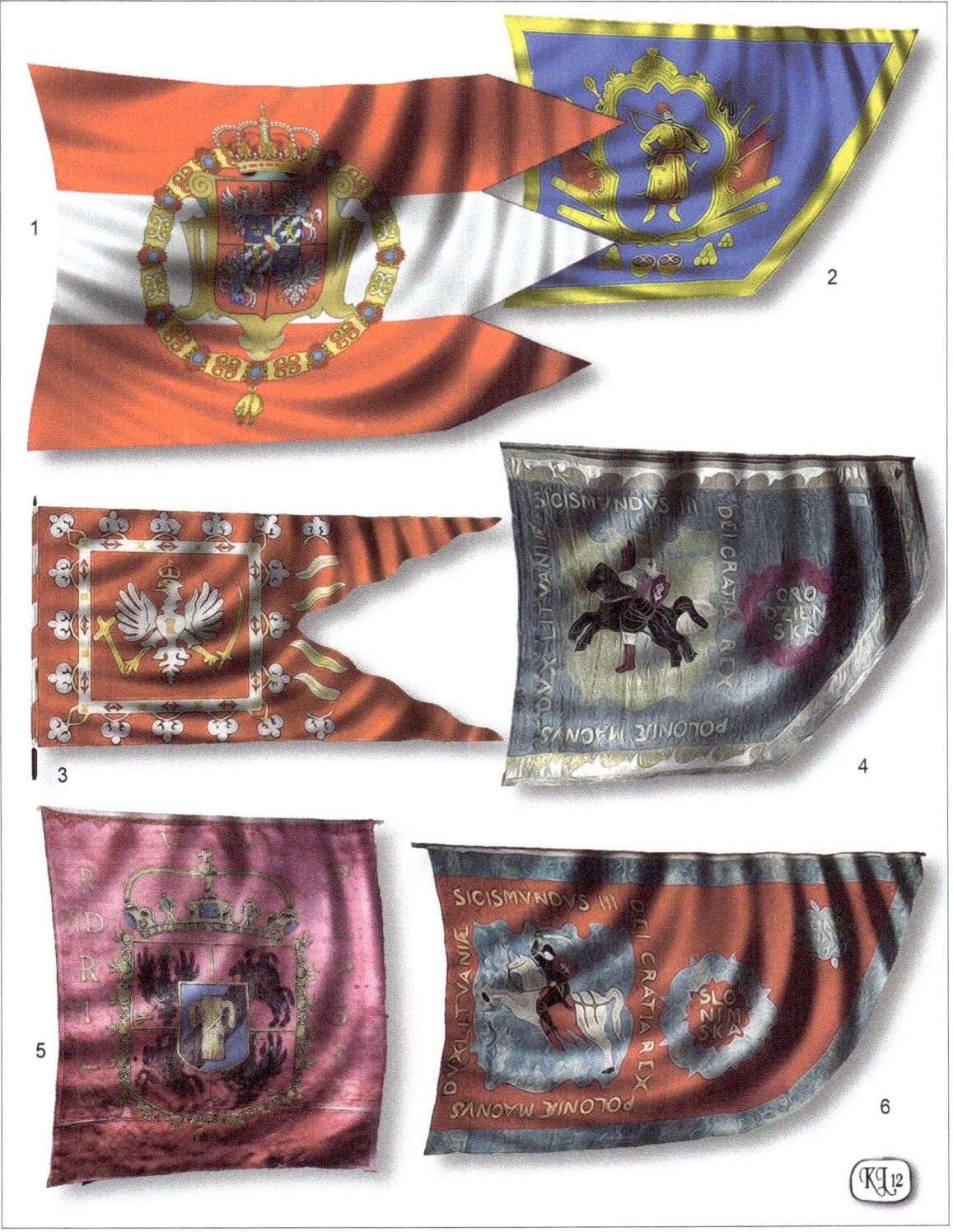

▲ Polish-Lithuanian flags and banners 1 Polish-Lithuanian Commonwea_th Coat of Arms. 2 Cossack Hetmanate Coat of Arms. 3 Kingdom of Poland Coat of Arms. 4 Banner of the Grodno's militia (aa. 1613-1619) – Museum Wojska Polskiego of Warsaw. 5 Banner of Wladislaw IV's trabants of the Royal Guard – Ibidem. 6 Banner of the Slonimski's militia (aa. 1613-1619) – Ibidem.

▲ Jan Sobieski, king of Poland.

APPENDIX, WHO'S WHO

WHO IS JOHN III SOBIESKI KING OF POLAND

John III Sobieski (17 August 1629 – 17 June 1696) was one of the most notable monarchs of the Polish–Lithuanian Commonwealth, from 1674 until his death King of Poland and Grand Duke of Lithuania. Sobieski's 22-year-reign was marked by a period of the Commonwealth's stabilization, much needed after the turmoil of the Deluge and Khmelnytsky Uprising. Very popular among his subjects, he was an able military commander, most famous for the victory over the Turks in the 1683 Battle of Vienna.

Following his victories over the Ottoman Empire, he was called by the Turks the *"Lion of Lechistan"*.

Sobieski's greatest success his naturally the victory at the Battle of Vienna, in joint command of Polish, Austrian and German troops, against the invading Turks under Kara Mustafa. Upon reaching Vienna, Sobieski had planned to attack on 13 September, but with the Turkish army close to breaching the walls he ordered a full attack on 12 September. At 4 am, the united army of about 81,000 men attacked a Turkish force of about 130,000 men. At about 5 pm, after observing the infantry battle from the hilltop, Sobieski led Polish husaria cavalry along with Austrians and Germans into a massive charge down the hillside.

Soon, the Turkish battle line was broken and the Ottoman forces scattered in confusion. At 5:30 pm Sobieski entered the deserted tent of Kara Mustafa and the battle of Vienna ended. The Pope and other foreign dignitaries hailed Sobieski as the"Savior of Vienna and Western European civilization.

In a letter to his wife he wrote *"All the common people kissed my hands, my feet, my clothes; others only touched me, saying: 'Ah, let us kiss so valiant a hand!'"*

Chara Musta: Tha Türckischer Groß Vezier welcher Anno 1683 den 12 Fülÿ die kaÿ: Residenz Statt Wien Belagert aber Swider den 12 Er: mit verlust vnd großen Spott Dheck geschlagen Worden

▲ Merzifonlu Kara Mustafa Pasha

WHO IS KARA MUSTAFA

Merzifonlu Kara Mustafa Pasha (1634 – 25 December 1683) was an Ottoman military leader and grand vizier who was a central character in the Ottoman Empire's last attempts at expansion into both Central and Eastern Europe. Born to Turkish parents in Merzifon, he married into the powerful Köprülü family and served as a messenger to Damascus for his brother-in-law, the grand vizier Köprülü Fazıl Ahmed Pasha.

He directed in the name of Köprülü family's mukata or tımar fields in Merzifon. After distinguishing himself, Mustafa became a vizier in his own right, and by 1663 or 1666 became the Kapudan Pasha (Grand Admiral of the Ottoman Navy). He served as a commander of ground troops in a war against Poland in 1672, negotiating a settlement that added the province of Podolia to the empire.

The victory enabled the Ottomans to transform the Cossack regions of the southern Ukraine into a protectorate. In 1676, when his brother-in-law Köprülü Fazıl Ahmed Pasha died, Mustafa succeeded him as grand vizier. He was less successful in combating a Cossack rebellion that began in 1678.

After some initial victories, intervention by Russia turned the tide and forced the Turks to conclude peace in 1681, effectively returning the Cossack lands to Russian rule with the exception of a few forts on the Dnieper and Southern Bug rivers. In 1683, he launched a campaign northward into Austria in a last effort to expand the Ottoman empire after more than 150 years of war. By mid-July, his 100,000-man army had besieged Vienna (guarded by 10,000 Habsburg soldiers), following in the footsteps of Suleiman the Magnificent in 1529. By September, he had taken a portion of the walls and appeared to be on his way to victory.

But on 12 September 1683, a Polish army under King Jan Sobieski took advantage of dissent within the Turkish military command and poor disposition of his troops, winning the Battle of Vienna with a devastating flank attack led by Sobieski's Polish cavalry (Polish Hussars). The Turks retreated into Hungary, leaving the kingdom for retaking by the Austrians in 1686. The defeat cost Mustafa his position, and ultimately, his life. On 25 December 1683, Kara Mustafa was executed in Belgrade at the order of Mehmed IV.

He suffered death by strangulation with a silk cord, which was the capital punishment inflicted on high-ranking persons in the Ottoman Empire. His last words were, in effect *"Make sure you tie the knot right."* Mustafa's head was presented to Mehmed IV in a velvet bag.

▲ The Austrian Emperor Leopold I Habsburg paint by Benjamin von Block.

WHO IS LEOPOLD Ist EMPEROR

Leopold I (June 1640 – 5 May 1705) was Holy Roman Emperor, King of Hungary and Croatia and King of Bohemia.

The second son of Ferdinand III, Holy Roman Emperor, by his first wife, Maria Anna of Spain, Leopold became heir apparent in 1654 by the death of his elder brother Ferdinand IV. Elected Holy Roman Emperor in 1658, Leopold would rule as such until his death in 1705.

Leopold's reign is known for the conflicts with the Ottoman Empire in the east, and the rivalry with Louis XIV, a contemporary and first cousin, in the west. After more than a decade of warfare, Leopold emerged victorious from the Great Turkish War thanks to military talents of Prince Eugene of Savoy.

By the Treaty of Karlowitz, Leopold recovered almost all of the Kingdom of Hungary which had fallen under the Turkish yoke in the years after the 1526 Battle of Mohács. The Turkish sultan sent an enormous army into Austria early in 1683; this advanced almost unchecked to Vienna, which was besieged from July to September, while Leopold took refuge at Passau. Realizing the gravity of the situation somewhat tardily, some of the German princes, among them the electors of Saxony and Bavaria, led their contingents to the Imperial Army, which was commanded by the emperor's brother-in-law, Charles, duke of Lorraine, but the most redoubtable of Leopold's allies was the king of Poland, John Sobieski, who was already dreaded by the Turks.

BIBLIOGRAPHY

SOBIESKI, Jan; Zeller, Joachim (1974), *Listy do Marysienki*, Berlin.

SZEMBERG, Teofil (1621), *Relacya prawdziwa o weszciu woyska polskiego do Wołoch y o potrzebie iego z pogaństwem w R. P. 1620 we wrześniu y w październiku*, Cracovia.

SZYMANOWSKI, Samuel Hutor (1642), *Mars Sauromatski, to jest od szczęśliwej koronacyjej Naiaśniejszego Władyslawa IV, z łaski Bożej króla polskiego etc. krótkie opisanie różnych ekspedycyj Jaśnie Oświeconemu Ksiażeciu J.M. Jeremiemu Michałowi Korybutowi, książęciu na Wiśniowcu Wiśniowieckiemu, Panu swemu Mciwemu, wydany przez Samuela Hutora Szymonowskiego z Kleczan*, Varsavia.

THOUR, Jacques-Auguste : de (1604), *Historiae sui temporis*, Paris.

CANTEMIR, Demetrio (1714-1716), *Descriptio Moldaviae*, ed. (1769), Berlin.

CANTEMIR, Demetrio (1714-1716), *Incrementa atque decrementa aulae othomanicae*, ed. *History of the Growth and Decay of the Ottoman Empire* (1734), London

COYER, Gabriel François (1761), *Histoire de Jean Sobieski, roi de Pologne*, Parigi, Duchesne.

GUER, Jean (1747), *Moeurs et Usages des Turcs*, Paris

MARSIGLI, Luigi Ferdinando (1732), *Stato Militare dell'Imperio Ottomano*, Amsterdam.

SCHÉRER, Jean Benoît (1789),*Geschichte der ukrainischen und saporogischen Kasaken*, Leipzig.

OTTOMAN EMPIRE:

AGOSTON, Gabor (2005), *Guns for the Sultan : military power and the weapons industry in the Ottoman Empire*, Cambridge University Press.

AYN-I, Ali (1864), *Risale-i Vazife-Horan*, Istanbul.

BENT, J. Theodore [a cura di] (1893), *Early voyages and travels in the Levant*, London.

CEVAD, Ahmed Beg (1882), *Etat Militaire Ottoman depuis la Fondation de l'Empire jusqu'à nos jours*, Istanbul.

GOFFMANN, Daniel (2004), *The Ottoman Empire and Early Modern Europe*, Cambridge University Press.

HAMMER, Johann : de (1828-31), *Storia dell'Impero ottomano*, Venezia, Antonelli, 24 v.

İNALCIK, Halil (1998), *The Question of the Closing of the Black Sea under the Ottomans*, in AAVV (1998), *Essays in Ottoman History*, Istanbul, Eren, pp. 415-45.

İNALCIK, Halil (1998), *Essays in Ottoman History*, Istanbul, Eren Yayıncılık.

İNALCIK, Halil (1995), *Fatih Devri Üzerinde Tetkikler ve Vesikalar*, Ankara, Türk Tarih Kurumu Yayınları.

İNALCIK, Halil (1994), *The Ottoman Empire: The Classical Age, 1300-1600*, Londra, Phoenix.

İNALCIK, Halil (1994), *An Economic and Social History of the Ottoman Empire, 1300-1914*, Cambridge Uni. Press.

İNALCIK, Halil (1983), *The Khan and the Tribal Aristocracy: the Crimean Khanate Under Sahib Giray I*, in *Emel* 135 (1983), pp. 74-96.

İNALCIK, Halil (1960), *The Encyclopaedia of Islam*, Leida.

İNALCIK, Halil (1948), *Osmanlı-Rus Rekabetinin Menşei ve Don-Volga Kanalı Teşebbüsü*, in *Belleten* 46/12 (1948), pp. 349-402.

İNALCIK, Halil (1944), *Yeni Vesikalara Göre Kırım Hanlığının Osmanlı Tâbiliğine Girmesi ve Ahidname Meselesi*, in *Belleten* 30/8 (Nisan 1944), pp. 185-229.

K.U.K.KRIEGSARCHIV (1874), *Feldzüge des Prinzen Eugen von Savoyen*, Vienna, vv. I, II, XVI e XVII – ed. (1880), Torino, Regio Stato Maggiore.

KINROSS, Patrick (1977), *The Ottoman Centuries : The Rise and Fall of the Turkish Empire*, London, Perennial.

KÜÇÜKYALÇIN, Erdal (2007), *Janissary and samurai : early modern warrior classes and religion*, tesi di laurea della Boğaziçi University.

MANTRAN, Robert (2005), *L'Empire Ottoman du XVI au XVIII siècle*, Parigi, Fayard.

MUGNAI, Bruno [e] Secco, Alberto (2011-2012), *La guerra di Candia : 1645-69*, Zanica, Soldiershop g. 2 v.

MUGNAI, Bruno (1998), *L'esercito ottomano da Candia a Passarowitz (1645-1718)*, Venezia, Filippi, 2 v.

MURPHEY, Rhoads (1999), *Ottoman Warfare, 1500-1700*, London, UCL Press.

ZIGULSKI, Zdizislaw Jr. (1992), *Ottoman Art in the service of the Empire*, New York University Press.

ZIGULSKI, Zdizislaw Jr. (1968), *Choragwie Tureckie w Polsce*, Cracovia.

POLISH ARMY:

BRZEZINSKI, Richard; [ill.] Velimir Vuksic (2005), *Polish winged hussar, 1500-1775*, Oxford, Osprey Publishing.

CHRZĄSZCZ, J. (1894), *Pierwszy okres buntu Chmielnickiego w oswietleniu uczestnika wyprawy Zoltowodzkiej : Prace historyczne w 30-lecie dzialanosci prof. St. Zakrzewskiego*, Leopoli.

DŁUGOŁĘCKI, Wojciech Jacek (2008), *Batoh 1652*, Varsavia, Bellona.

MILLAR, Simon ; [ill.] Dennis, Peter (2008), *Vienna 1683 : Christian Europe Repels the Ottomans*, Oxford, Osprey Publishing.

PODHORODECKI, Leszek (2008), *Chocim 1621*, Varsavia, Bellona.

PODHORODECKI, Leszek (2001), *Wiedeń 1683*, Varsavia, Bellona.

PODHORODECKI, Leszek (1978), Stanisław *Koniecpolski ok. 1592–1646*, Varsavia,

ROMAŃSKI, Romuald (2008), *Beresteczko 1651*, Varsavia, Bellona.

SZCZEŚNIAK, Robert (2001), *Kluszyn 1610*, Varsavia, Bellona.

SIKORA, Radoslaw (2007), *Chocim (Khotyn) 1621*, ed. on-line su www.republika.pl

SIKORSKI, Michał (2007), *Wyprawa Sobieskiego na czambuly tatarskie 1672*, Inforteditions.

SIKORSKI, Janusz (1990), *Polskie tradycje wojskowe*, Varsavia, MON, t. I.

ŚLEDZIŃSKI, Kacper (2007), *Cecora 1620*, Varsavia, Bellona.

ŚLEDZIŃSKI, Kacper (2005), *Zbaraż 1649*, Varsavia, Bellona.

SULIMIERSKI, Filip; Chlebowski, Bronisław; Walewski, Władysław (1880-1902), *Słownik geograficzny Królestwa Polskiego* [Dizionario geografico del Regno di Polonia], Varsavia.

WASILEWSKI, Witold (2002), *Wyprawa bukowinska Stanislawa Jablonowskiego w 1685 roku*, Varsavia.

WOJTASIK, Janusz (1990), *Podhajce 1698*, Varsavia, Bellona.

OTHER BOOK:

DOMAR, Evsey D. (1989), *Capitalism, socialism, and serfdom: essays*, Cambridge University Press.

FAROQHI, Suraiya N. [a cura di] (2006), *The Latter Ottoman Empire*, Cambridge University Press.

JABLONOWSKI, H. (1978), *La Polonia sino alla morte di Giovanni Sobieski*, in CARSTEN, F.L. (1978), *Storia del Mondo Moderno : V, La supremazic della Francia (1648-1688)*, Milano, Garzanti, pp. 721-736.

JABLONOWSKI, H. (1971), *La fine dell'espansione polacca e la sopravvivenza della Russia : I, Polonia-Lituania: 1609-48*, in COOPER, J.P. [a cura di] (1971), *Storia del Mondo Moderno : IV, La decadenza della Spagna e la Guerra dei trent'anni (1610-1648/59)*, Milano, Garzanti, pp. 686-704.

KOŁODZIEJCZYK, Dariusz (2000), *Ottoman-Polish diplomatic relations (15th-18th century) : an annotated edition of 'ahdnames and other documents*, Leida-Boston, Brill.

KURAT, A.N. (1978), *L'impero ottomano sotto Maometto IV*, in CARSTEN, F.L., *Op. Cit.*, pp. 645-669.

PACH, Zsigmond Pál (1970), *The role of East-Central Europe in international trade, 16th and 17th centuries*, Akadémiai Kiadó.

PARRY, V.J. (1968), *L'impero ottomano dal 1617 al 1648*, in COOPER, J.P., *Op. Cit.*, pp. 726-749.

PARRY, V.J. (1968), *L'impero ottomano (1566-1617)*, in WERNHAM, R.B. [a cura di] (1968), *Storia del Mondo Moderno : III, La controriforma e la rivoluzione dei prezzi (1599-1610)*, Milano, Garzanti, pp. 452-484.

PLATANIA, G. (2000), *Rzeczpospolita, Europa e Santa Sede tra intese ed ostilità. Saggi sulla Polonia* Viterbo.

SKWARCZYŃSKI, P. (1968), *La Polonia e la Lituania*, in WERNHAM, R.B., *Op. Cit.*, pp. 485-517.

WARZYNIAK, Krzysztof (2003), *Ottoman-Polish diplomatic relations in the Sixteenth Century*, Ankara.

WITNESS TO HISTORY

Our new series of books of history, based on eyewitnesses, or the great storytellers and war correspondents of the great events of world history: battles, sieges, military campaigns, but also travels and discoveries. New books from old books, completely revised and illustrated by Soldiershop! Our edition, the first ever published in English, available both on paperback and digital format, richly illustrated with unpublished and colored plates.

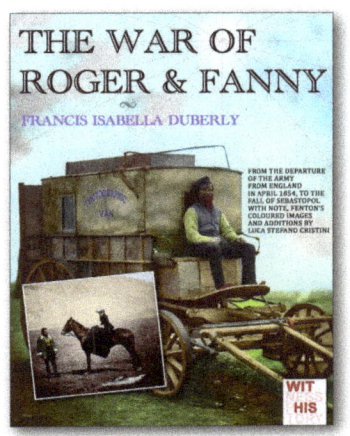

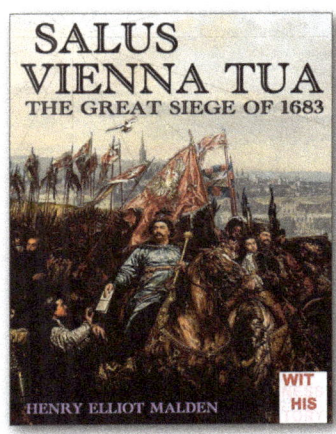

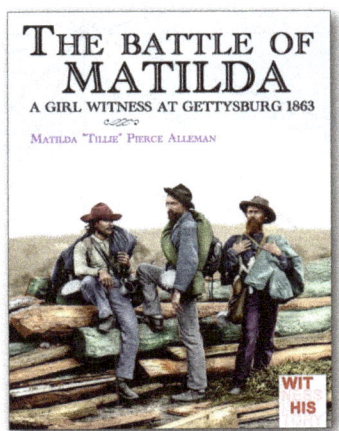

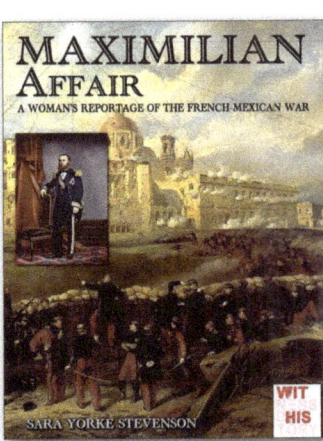

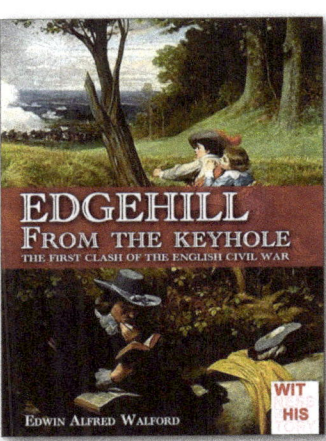